Contents

Topic	Page
1 Patterning and Grouping	2-7
2 Investigating Addition	8-11
3 Addition Strategies *near doubles*	12-15
4 Measurement — *using standard units for length, capacity*	16
5 Investigating Tens and Ones	17-22
6 Two-Digit Numbers & Hundreds	23-26
7 Investigating Subtraction	27-31
8 Subtraction Strategies	32-35
9 Investigating Solid Shapes	36-37
10 Visual Representation *graphing*	38-40
11 Addition Strategies *using tens*	41-43
12 Exploring Addition of Two-Digit Numbers	44-45
13 Measurement — *using standard units for weight*	46-47
14 Introducing More Plane Shapes	48-49
15 Subtraction Strategies *near doubles*	50-54
16 Exploring Subtraction of Two-Digit Numbers	55-56

Topic	Page
17 Hundreds, Tens, and Ones	57-59
18 Place Value with Three-Digit Numbers	60-64
19 Money *using new coins*	65-70
20 Multiplication *introducing formal language*	71-76
21 Time *five-minute intervals*	77-80
22 Division *using informal language*	81-84
23 Measurement *relating units involving length*	85-87
24 Extending the Addition Algorithm	88-93
25 Investigating Plane Shapes	94-97
26 More Subtraction Strategies	98-99
27 Extending the Subtraction Algorithm	100-104
28 Fractions and Area *halves, thirds, fourths*	105-108
29 Extending Multiplication and Division	109-112
Index	*Inside back cover*

Name _____

In each picture, color 16 squares to make a design.
Use 2 colors.

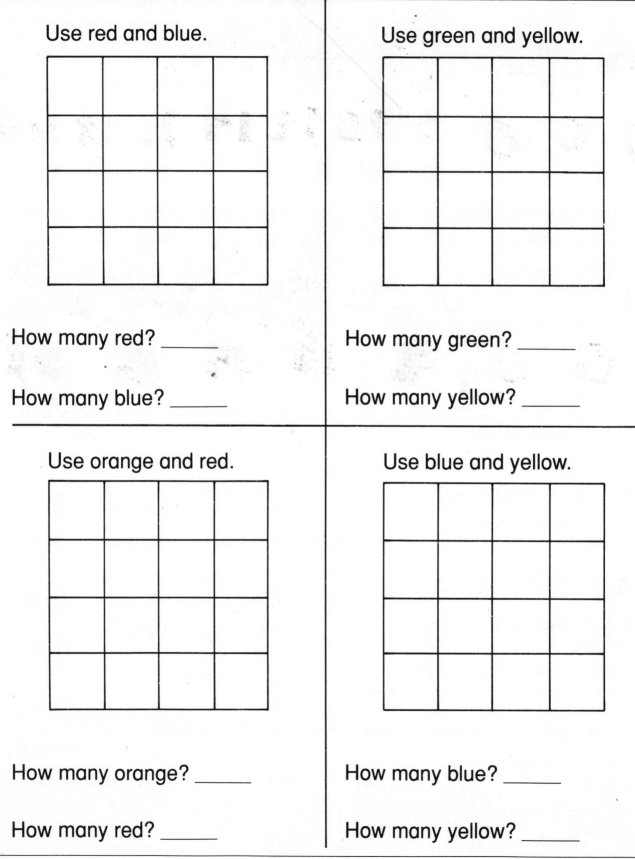

Use red and blue.

How many red? _____

How many blue? _____

Use green and yellow.

How many green? _____

How many yellow? _____

Use orange and red.

How many orange? _____

How many red? _____

Use blue and yellow.

How many blue? _____

How many yellow? _____

2

Name _____

1. Color the squares to make a pattern of twos.
   Count by twos. Write the numbers.

2   4   6   _8_   _10_   _12_   _14_   _16_   _18_   _20_

2. Color the circles to make a pattern of threes.
   Count by threes. Write the numbers.

3   6   ____   ____   _15_   _18_   _21_

3. Color the triangles to make a pattern of fours.
   Count by fours. Write the numbers.

___   ___   ___   ___   ___

4. Draw a pattern of fives. Write the numbers.

___   ___   ___   ___   ___   ___

Name _____

1. Write the missing numbers in each picture.

2. Ring all the even numbers.

3. Color the last number in each row.

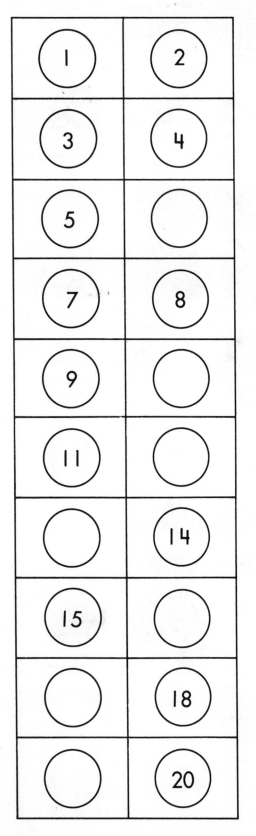

1	2	3
4	5	
7		
10		
13	14	
	17	

1		2		3			
5		6		7		8	
9		10					
13							
		18					

4

Name _Krystal_

1. Color coins to show each amount.
2. Write the amount you did not color.

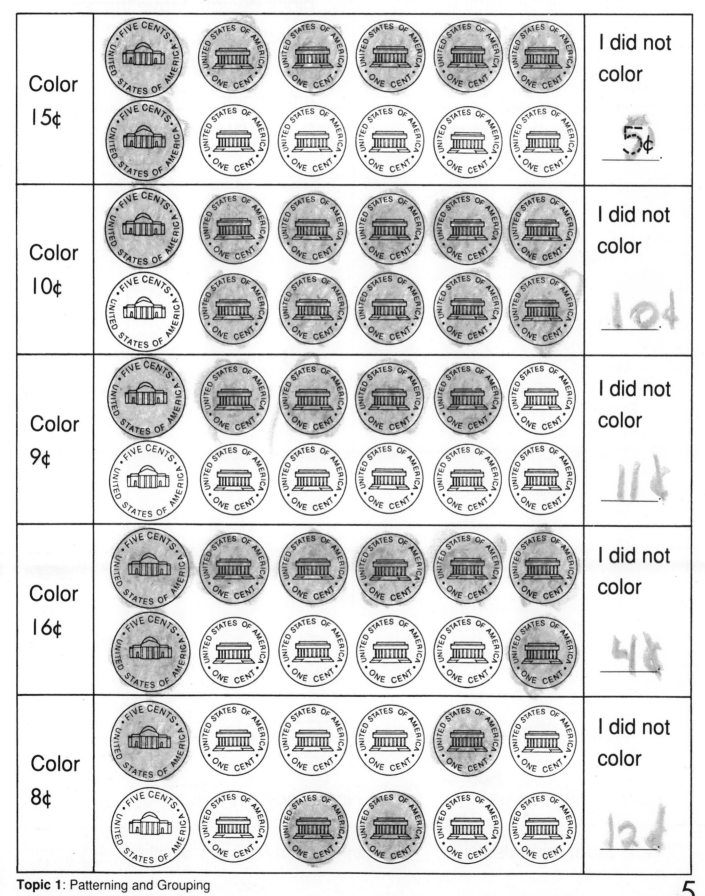

Color 15¢		I did not color 5¢
Color 10¢		I did not color 10¢
Color 9¢		I did not color 11¢
Color 16¢		I did not color 4¢
Color 8¢		I did not color 12¢

Topic 1: Patterning and Grouping

5

Name _____

1. Color all the squares orange.
   Color all the triangles green.
   Color all the diamonds blue.

Block   Design

2. Put pattern blocks on the
   block design. Move the blocks
   to make a graph.
   Trace around
   the blocks.

Block   Graph

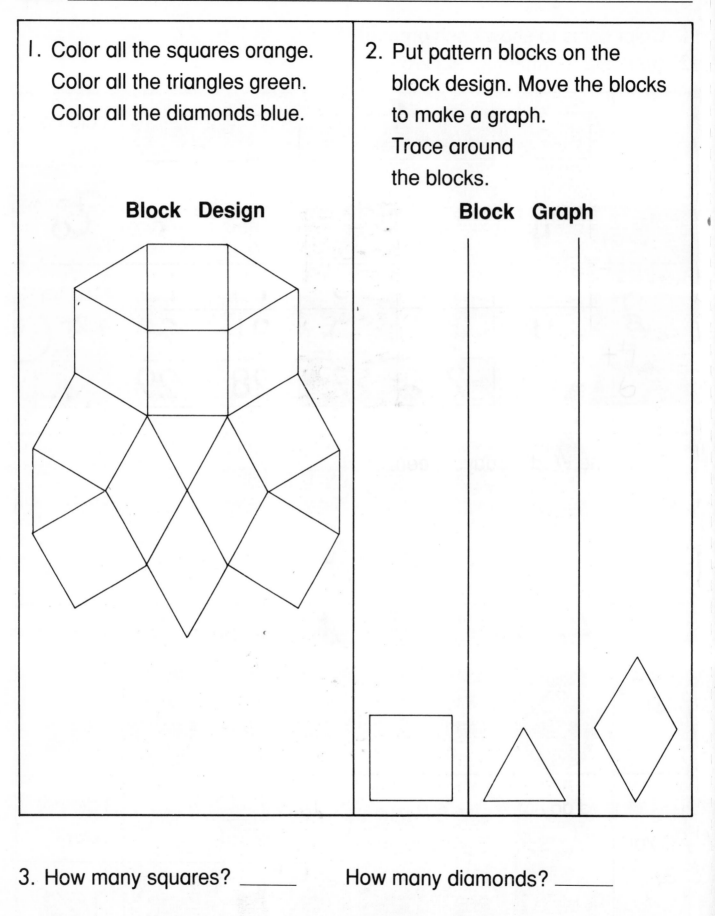

3. How many squares? _____   How many diamonds? _____

   How many triangles?_____   How many blocks in all? _____

Name _Krystal-Ann Lord_

1. Write the names of the days of the week.

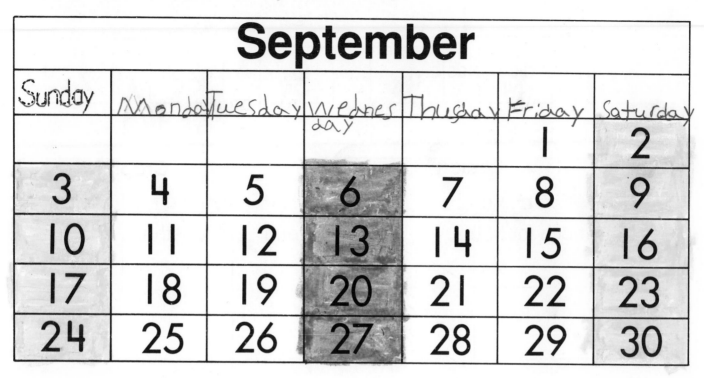

Sunday	Monday	Tuesday	Wednesday	Thursday	Friday	Saturday
					1	2
3	4	5	6	7	8	9
10	11	12	13	14	15	16
17	18	19	20	21	22	23
24	25	26	27	28	29	30

2. Color the Wednesdays green.

3. Color the weekends yellow.

4. Write the dates that are Fridays.

____1____ ____8____ ___15___ ___22___ ___29___

5. Write the names of these days.

The first day of the month ___Friday___

The third day of the month ___Sunday___

The tenth day of the month ___Sunday___

The last day of the month ___Saturday___

Topic 1: Patterning and Grouping

7

Name **Krystal-Ann Lord**

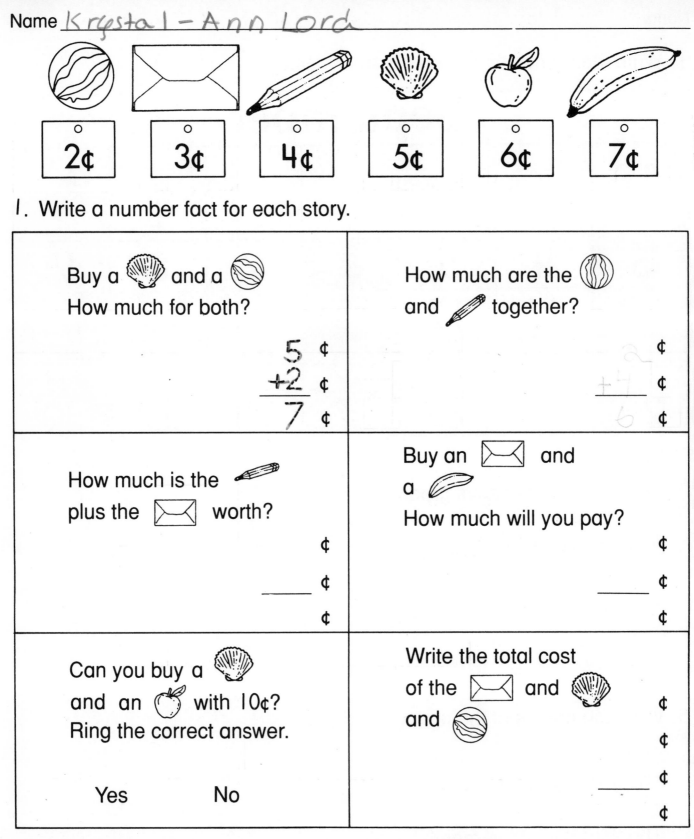

2¢   3¢   4¢   5¢   6¢   7¢

1. Write a number fact for each story.

Buy a 🐚 and a 🍉 How much for both? $\begin{array}{r} 5 \\ +2 \\ \hline 7 \end{array}$ ¢ ¢ ¢	How much are the 🍉 and ✏ together? ___ ¢ ___ ¢ ___ ¢
How much is the ✏ plus the ✉ worth? ___ ¢ ___ ¢ ___ ¢	Buy an ✉ and a 🍌 How much will you pay? ___ ¢ ___ ¢ ___ ¢
Can you buy a 🐚 and an 🍎 with 10¢? Ring the correct answer. Yes No	Write the total cost of the ✉ and 🐚 and 🍉 ___ ¢ ___ ¢ ___ ¢ ___ ¢

2. Write the answers. Keep on going with the pattern.

$\begin{array}{r} 9 \\ +1 \\ \hline \end{array}$ $\begin{array}{r} 8 \\ +2 \\ \hline \end{array}$ $\begin{array}{r} 7 \\ +3 \\ \hline \end{array}$ $\begin{array}{r} \\ + \\ \hline \end{array}$ $\begin{array}{r} \\ + \\ \hline \end{array}$ $\begin{array}{r} \\ + \\ \hline \end{array}$ $\begin{array}{r} \\ + \\ \hline \end{array}$ $\begin{array}{r} \\ + \\ \hline \end{array}$

Name _____

1. Write the count-on 1, 2, and 3 facts
   for each of these cards. Draw dots to help.

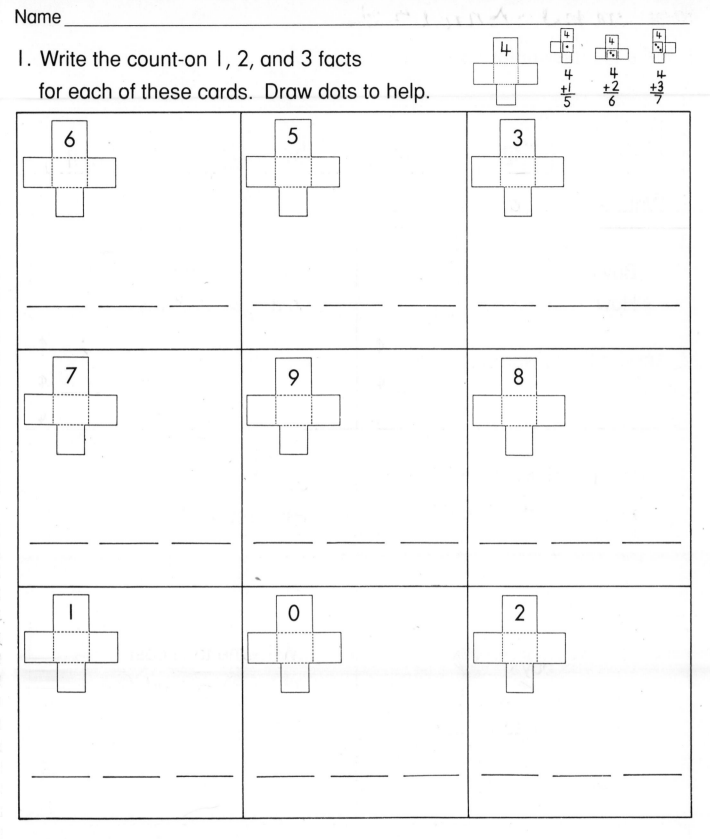

4   4   4   4
    +1   +2   +3
    5   6   7

6	5	3
___ ___ ___ ___	___ ___ ___ ___	___ ___ ___ ___
7	9	8
___ ___ ___ ___	___ ___ ___ ___	___ ___ ___ ___
1	0	2
___ ___ ___ ___	___ ___ ___ ___	___ ___ ___ ___

2. Write the answers. Keep the pattern going.

   0   1   2   3
  +0   +0   +0   +0   ___   ___   ___   ___

Name __Krystal-Ann Lordom__

1. Write the answer for each fact.

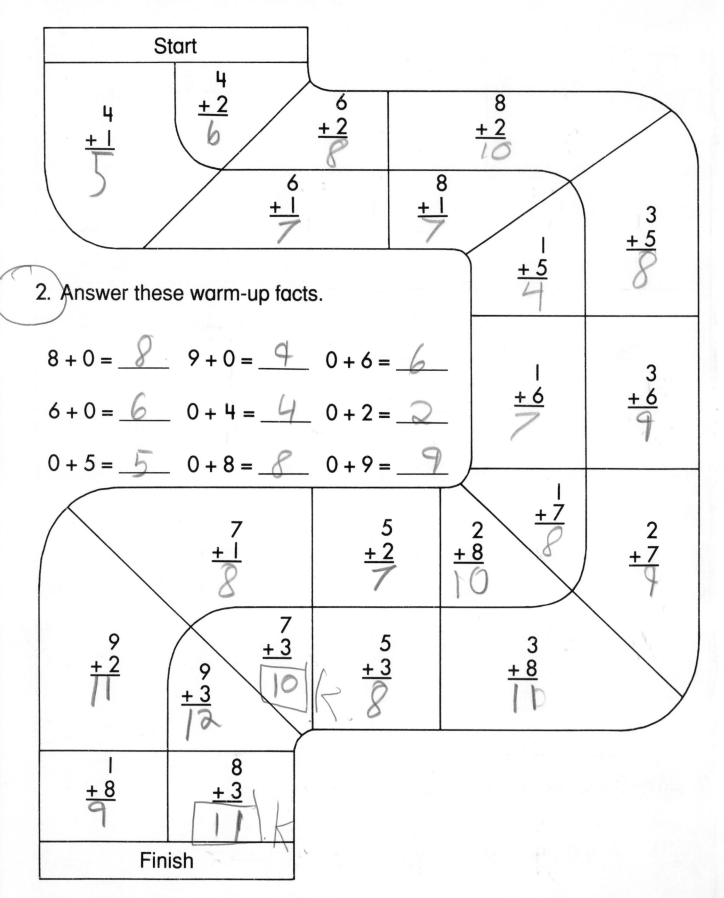

Start

$\begin{array}{r} 4 \\ +1 \\ \hline 5 \end{array}$

$\begin{array}{r} 4 \\ +2 \\ \hline 6 \end{array}$

$\begin{array}{r} 6 \\ +2 \\ \hline 8 \end{array}$

$\begin{array}{r} 8 \\ +2 \\ \hline 10 \end{array}$

$\begin{array}{r} 6 \\ +1 \\ \hline 7 \end{array}$

$\begin{array}{r} 8 \\ +1 \\ \hline 7 \end{array}$

$\begin{array}{r} 1 \\ +5 \\ \hline 4 \end{array}$

$\begin{array}{r} 3 \\ +5 \\ \hline 8 \end{array}$

$\begin{array}{r} 1 \\ +6 \\ \hline 7 \end{array}$

$\begin{array}{r} 3 \\ +6 \\ \hline 9 \end{array}$

$\begin{array}{r} 1 \\ +7 \\ \hline 8 \end{array}$

2. Answer these warm-up facts.

$8 + 0 = \underline{8}$ $9 + 0 = \underline{4}$ $0 + 6 = \underline{6}$

$6 + 0 = \underline{6}$ $0 + 4 = \underline{4}$ $0 + 2 = \underline{2}$

$0 + 5 = \underline{5}$ $0 + 8 = \underline{8}$ $0 + 9 = \underline{9}$

$\begin{array}{r} 7 \\ +1 \\ \hline 8 \end{array}$

$\begin{array}{r} 5 \\ +2 \\ \hline 7 \end{array}$

$\begin{array}{r} 2 \\ +8 \\ \hline 10 \end{array}$

$\begin{array}{r} 2 \\ +7 \\ \hline 9 \end{array}$

$\begin{array}{r} 9 \\ +2 \\ \hline 11 \end{array}$

$\begin{array}{r} 9 \\ +3 \\ \hline 12 \end{array}$

$\begin{array}{r} 7 \\ +3 \\ \hline 10 \end{array}$

$\begin{array}{r} 5 \\ +3 \\ \hline 8 \end{array}$

$\begin{array}{r} 3 \\ +8 \\ \hline 11 \end{array}$

$\begin{array}{r} 1 \\ +8 \\ \hline 9 \end{array}$

$\begin{array}{r} 8 \\ +3 \\ \hline 11 \end{array}$

Finish

10

Topic 2: Investigating Addition

Name _Krystal-Ann Lordon_

1. Draw a picture to show each double.
   Then write the addition fact.

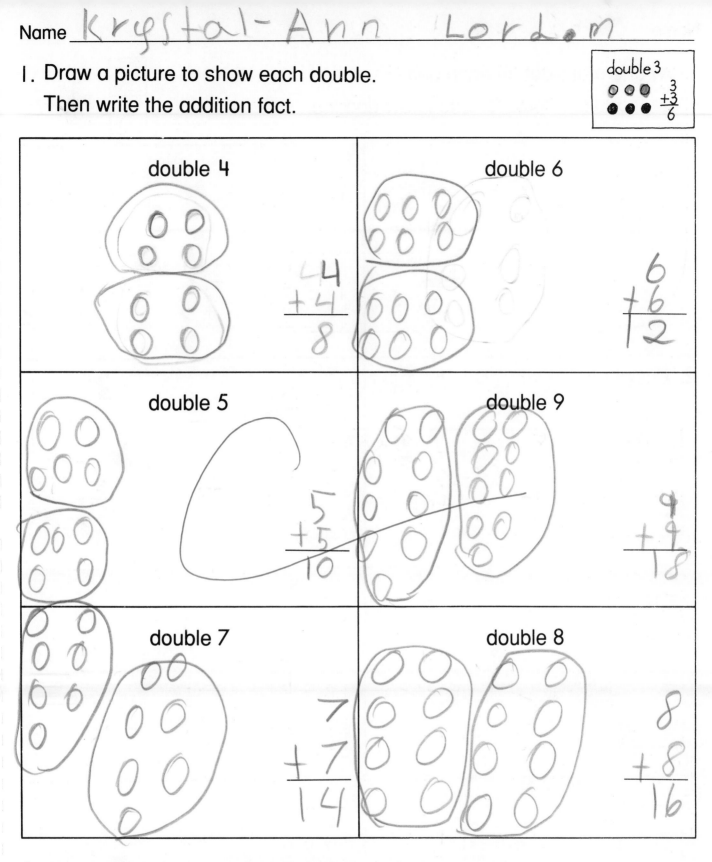

double 4

$$\begin{array}{r} 4 \\ +4 \\ \hline 8 \end{array}$$

double 6

$$\begin{array}{r} 6 \\ +6 \\ \hline 2 \end{array}$$

double 5

$$\begin{array}{r} 5 \\ +5 \\ \hline 10 \end{array}$$

double 9

$$\begin{array}{r} 9 \\ +9 \\ \hline 18 \end{array}$$

double 7

$$\begin{array}{r} 7 \\ +7 \\ \hline 14 \end{array}$$

double 8

$$\begin{array}{r} 8 \\ +8 \\ \hline 16 \end{array}$$

double 3

$$\begin{array}{r} 3 \\ +3 \\ \hline 6 \end{array}$$

2. How far can you double? Keep the pattern going.

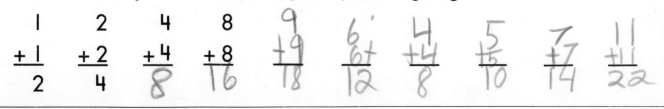

$$\begin{array}{r} 1 \\ +1 \\ \hline 2 \end{array} \quad \begin{array}{r} 2 \\ +2 \\ \hline 4 \end{array} \quad \begin{array}{r} 4 \\ +4 \\ \hline 8 \end{array} \quad \begin{array}{r} 8 \\ +8 \\ \hline 16 \end{array} \quad \begin{array}{r} 9 \\ +9 \\ \hline 18 \end{array} \quad \begin{array}{r} 6 \\ +6 \\ \hline 12 \end{array} \quad \begin{array}{r} 4 \\ +4 \\ \hline 8 \end{array} \quad \begin{array}{r} 5 \\ +5 \\ \hline 10 \end{array} \quad \begin{array}{r} 7 \\ +7 \\ \hline 14 \end{array} \quad \begin{array}{r} 11 \\ +11 \\ \hline 22 \end{array}$$

Draw one more dot on each domino.
Write 2 addition facts for each new domino.

$$\begin{array}{c} 2 \\ +3 \\ \hline 5 \end{array} \quad \begin{array}{c} 3 \\ +2 \\ \hline 5 \end{array}$$

$$\begin{array}{c} 2 \\ +1 \\ \hline 3 \end{array} \quad \begin{array}{c} 1 \\ +2 \\ \hline 3 \end{array}$$

$$\begin{array}{c} 6 \\ +7 \\ \hline 13 \end{array} \quad \begin{array}{c} 7 \\ +6 \\ \hline 13 \end{array}$$

$$\begin{array}{c} 8 \\ +7 \\ \hline 15 \end{array} \quad \begin{array}{c} 7 \\ +8 \\ \hline 15 \end{array}$$

$$\begin{array}{c} 5 \\ +6 \\ \hline 11 \end{array} \quad \begin{array}{c} 6 \\ +5 \\ \hline 11 \end{array}$$

$$\begin{array}{c} 3 \\ +4 \\ \hline 7 \end{array} \quad \begin{array}{c} 4 \\ +3 \\ \hline 7 \end{array}$$

$$\begin{array}{c} 8 \\ +9 \\ \hline 17 \end{array} \quad \begin{array}{c} 9 \\ +8 \\ \hline 17 \end{array}$$

$$\begin{array}{c} 4 \\ +5 \\ \hline 9 \end{array} \quad \begin{array}{c} 5 \\ +4 \\ \hline 9 \end{array}$$

$$\begin{array}{c} 9 \\ +10 \\ \hline 19 \end{array} \quad \begin{array}{c} 10 \\ +9 \\ \hline 19 \end{array}$$

Topic 3: Addition Strategies - near doubles

Name _____

1. On each number strip, color the numbers you say to find the answer.
   Write the answers.

double 6 plus 1 is __13__

| 1 | 2 | 3 | 4 | 5 | 6 | 7 | 8 | 9 | 10 | 11 | 12 | 13 | 14 | 15 | 16 | 17 | 18 | 19 | 20 |

double 3 plus 1 is _____

| 1 | 2 | 3 | 4 | 5 | 6 | 7 | 8 | 9 | 10 | 11 | 12 | 13 | 14 | 15 | 16 | 17 | 18 | 19 | 20 |

double 5 plus 1 is _____

| 1 | 2 | 3 | 4 | 5 | 6 | 7 | 8 | 9 | 10 | 11 | 12 | 13 | 14 | 15 | 16 | 17 | 18 | 19 | 20 |

double 7 plus 1 is _____

| 1 | 2 | 3 | 4 | 5 | 6 | 7 | 8 | 9 | 10 | 11 | 12 | 13 | 14 | 15 | 16 | 17 | 18 | 19 | 20 |

double 4 plus 1 is _____

| 1 | 2 | 3 | 4 | 5 | 6 | 7 | 8 | 9 | 10 | 11 | 12 | 13 | 14 | 15 | 16 | 17 | 18 | 19 | 20 |

double 8 plus 1 is _____

| 1 | 2 | 3 | 4 | 5 | 6 | 7 | 8 | 9 | 10 | 11 | 12 | 13 | 14 | 15 | 16 | 17 | 18 | 19 | 20 |

2. Write the answers.

| 6   7 | 3   4 | 5   6 |
+7 +6	+4 +3	+6 +5
7 8	4 5	8 9
+8 +7	+5 +4	+9 +8

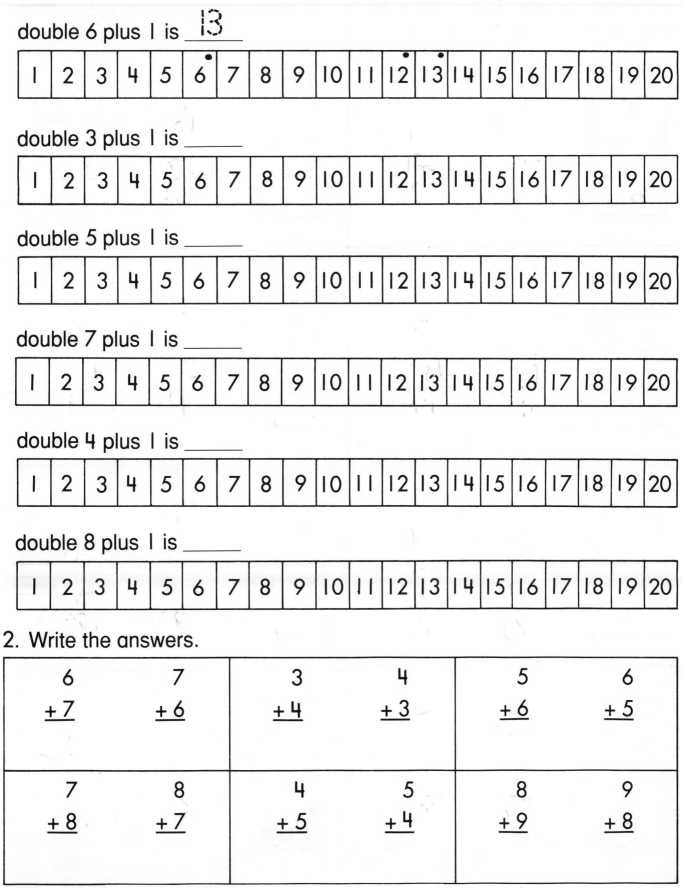

Topic 3: Addition Strategies - near doubles

13

Draw 2 more dots on one side of each domino.
Then write 2 addition facts for the new domino.

$\begin{array}{cc} 2 & 4 \\ +4 & +2 \\ \hline 6 & 6 \end{array}$

$\begin{array}{cc} 1 & 3 \\ +3 & +1 \\ \hline 4 & 4 \end{array}$

$\begin{array}{cc} 8 & 6 \\ +6 & +8 \\ \hline 14 & 14 \end{array}$

$\begin{array}{cc} 7 & 9 \\ +9 & +7 \\ \hline 16 & 16 \end{array}$

$\begin{array}{cc} 5 & 7 \\ +7 & +5 \\ \hline 12 & 12 \end{array}$

$\begin{array}{cc} 3 & 5 \\ +5 & +3 \\ \hline 8 & 8 \end{array}$

$\begin{array}{cc} 4 & 6 \\ +6 & +4 \\ \hline 10 & 10 \end{array}$

$\begin{array}{cc} 9 & 11 \\ +11 & +9 \\ \hline 20 & 20 \end{array}$

$\begin{array}{cc} 8 & 10 \\ +10 & 8 \\ \hline 18 & 18 \end{array}$

Topic 3: Addition Strategies - near doubles

Name _____

1. On each number strip, color the numbers you say to find the answer. Write the answers.

double 6 plus 2 is 14

| 1 | 2 | 3 | 4 | 5 | 6 | 7 | 8 | 9 | 10 | 11 | 12 | 13 | 14 | 15 | 16 | 17 | 18 | 19 | 20 |

double 3 plus 2 is _____

| 1 | 2 | 3 | 4 | 5 | 6 | 7 | 8 | 9 | 10 | 11 | 12 | 13 | 14 | 15 | 16 | 17 | 18 | 19 | 20 |

double 5 plus 2 is _____

| 1 | 2 | 3 | 4 | 5 | 6 | 7 | 8 | 9 | 10 | 11 | 12 | 13 | 14 | 15 | 16 | 17 | 18 | 19 | 20 |

double 7 plus 2 is _____

| 1 | 2 | 3 | 4 | 5 | 6 | 7 | 8 | 9 | 10 | 11 | 12 | 13 | 14 | 15 | 16 | 17 | 18 | 19 | 20 |

double 8 plus 2 is _____

| 1 | 2 | 3 | 4 | 5 | 6 | 7 | 8 | 9 | 10 | 11 | 12 | 13 | 14 | 15 | 16 | 17 | 18 | 19 | 20 |

double 4 plus 2 is _____

| 1 | 2 | 3 | 4 | 5 | 6 | 7 | 8 | 9 | 10 | 11 | 12 | 13 | 14 | 15 | 16 | 17 | 18 | 19 | 20 |

2. Write the answers.

6 + 8	8 + 6	3 + 5	5 + 3	5 + 7	7 + 5
9 + 7	7 + 9	4 + 6	6 + 4	8 + 10	10 + 8

Topic 3: Addition Strategies - near doubles

15

Name _____

1. Write how many different body parts you guess will fit along a meter stick.

2. Measure with a meter stick to check. Write the numbers.

Use words like "about," "almost" "between," "nearly"

My guess			My measure
	handspans		
	palms		
	footprints		
	cubits		

3. Write how many of each of these objects you guess will fit end-to-end along a meter stick.

4. Measure with a meter stick to check. Write the numbers.

My guess			My measure
	plastic cubes		
	yellow rods		
	pink rods		
	ones blocks		

Topic 4: Measurement - using standard units for length, capacity

Name Krystal-Ann Lordm.

1. Ring tens. Write the number of tens and ones.

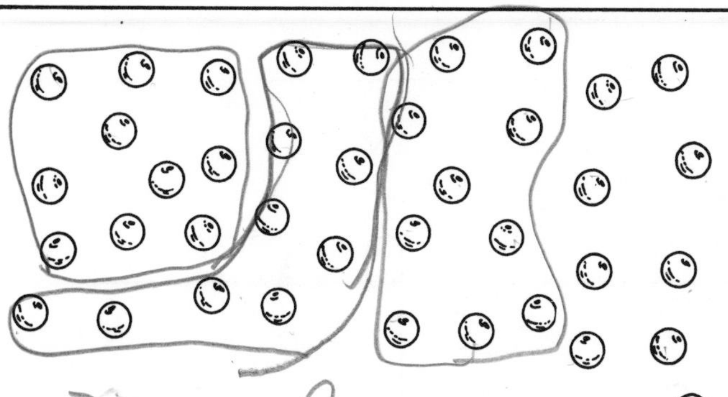

13 tens 9 ones

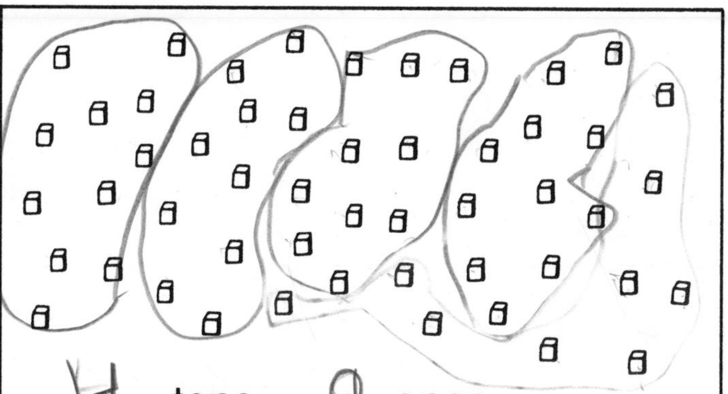

4 tens 9 ones

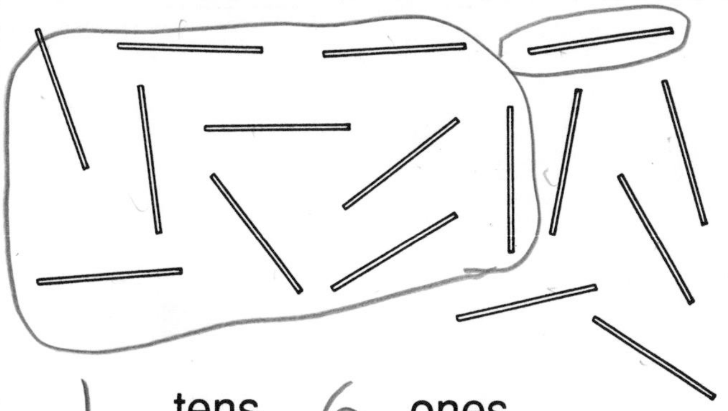

1 tens 6 ones

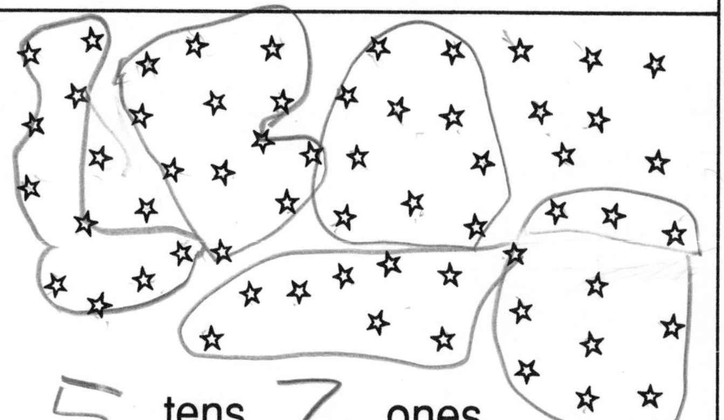

5 tens 7 ones

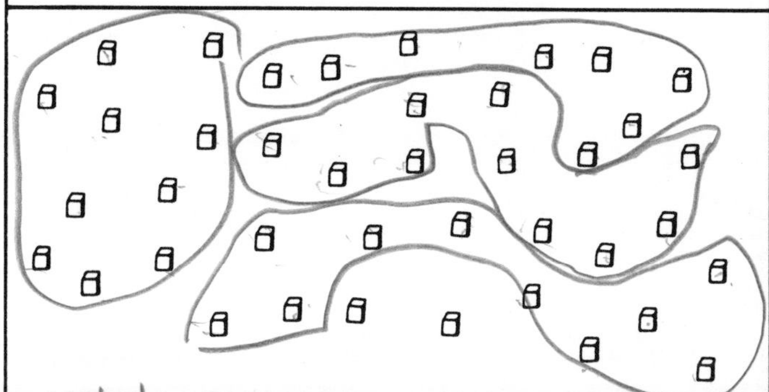

4 tens 1 ones

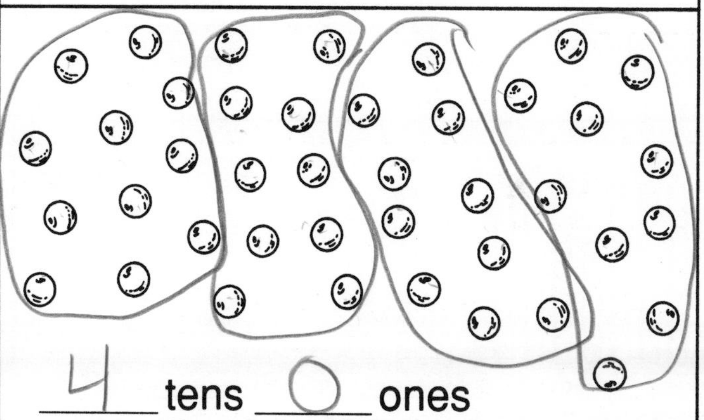

4 tens 0 ones

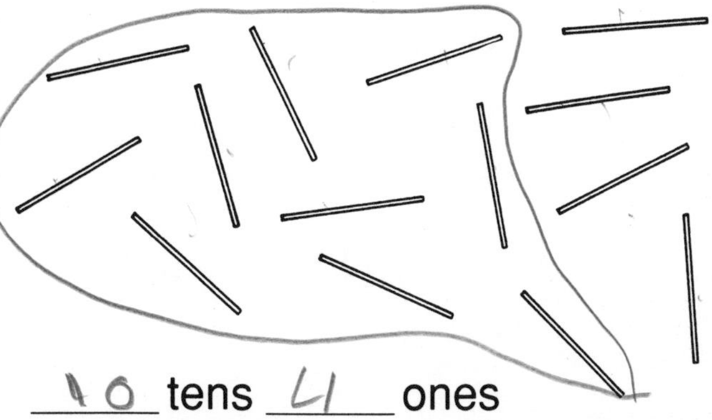

10 tens 4 ones

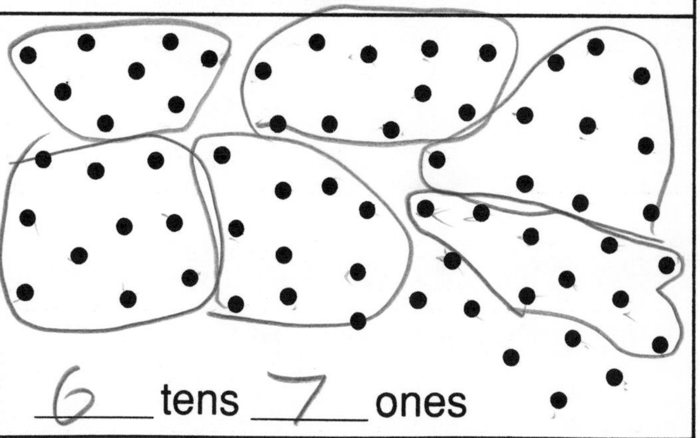

6 tens 7 ones

2. Mark each picture that is more than fifty.

Topic 5: Investigating Tens and Ones

17

Name _____

1. Look at each picture. Write the number of tens and ones.
   Then write the number word and the number.

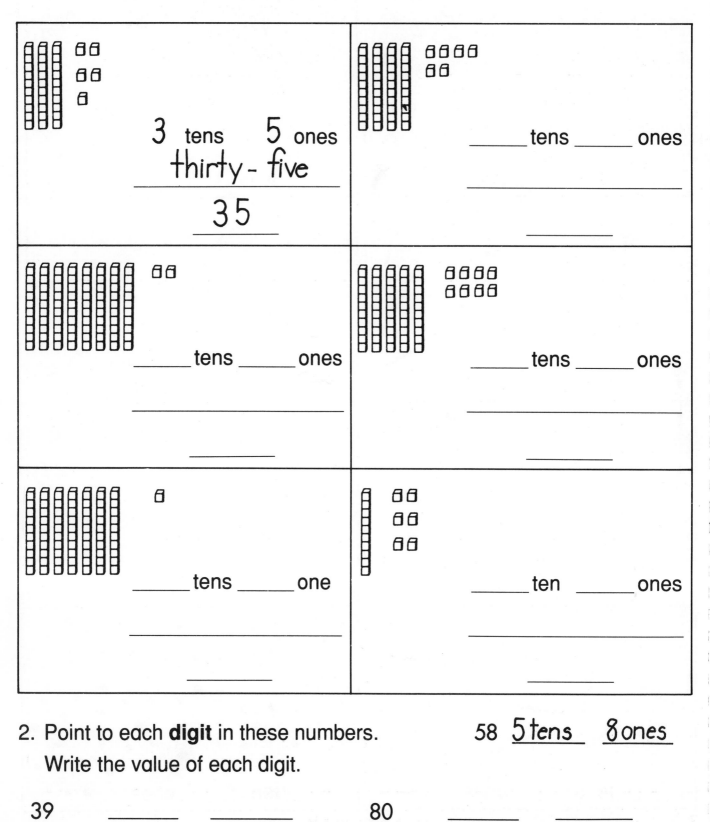

3 tens   5 ones
thirty - five
35

_____ tens _____ ones
_____
_____

_____ tens _____ ones
_____
_____

_____ tens _____ ones
_____
_____

_____ tens _____ one
_____
_____

_____ ten _____ ones
_____
_____

2. Point to each **digit** in these numbers.
   Write the value of each digit.

58 5 tens   8 ones

39 _____   _____   80 _____   _____

71 _____   _____   18 _____   _____

Topic 5: Investigating Tens and Ones

Name _____

1. Draw tens and ones blocks for each of these numbers.
   Write each number word.

85 _____	57 _____
86 _____	68 _____
80 _____	18 _____

2. Ring all the eights that are in the tens place.
   Underline all the eights that are in the ones place.

Name _____

1. Write the missing numbers on this number strip.

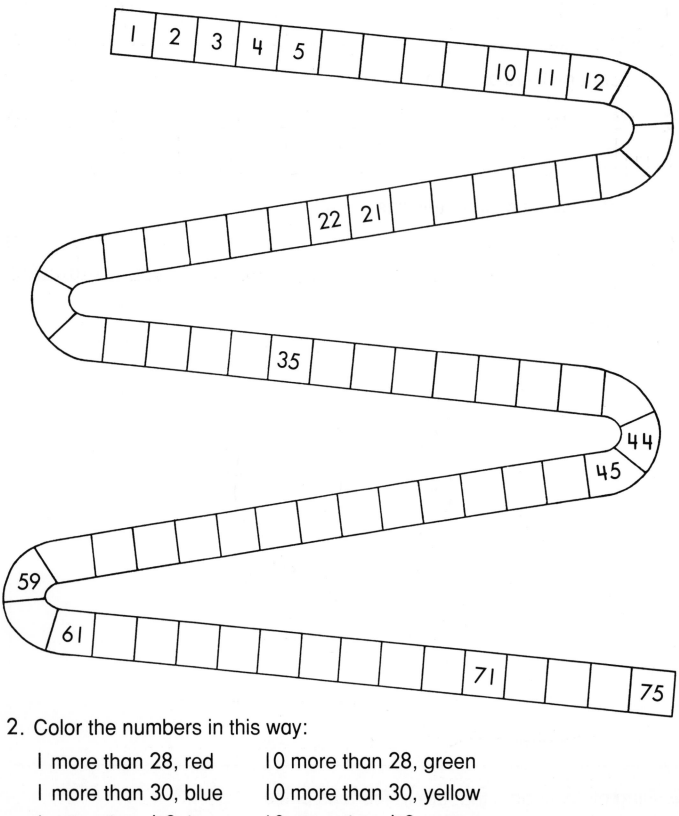

2. Color the numbers in this way:

I more than 28, red   10 more than 28, green

I more than 30, blue   10 more than 30, yellow

I more than 49, brown   10 more than 49, orange

Topic 5: Investigating Tens and Ones

Name _____

1. Write the missing numbers.

Count by ones along this line.

0   1   2   ___   4   ___   ___   ___   ___   ___   10   ___   12

Count by fives along this line.

0   5   10   15   ___   25   ___   ___   ___   ___   50   ___   60

Count by tens along this line.

0   10   ___   ___   ___   ___   ___   ___   ___   ___   100

2. Write the numbers on this clock.

12

3. Write the times.

I hour after 3 o'clock is _____

2 hours after 3 o'clock is _____

3 hours after 3 o'clock is _____

4 hours after 3 o'clock is _____

Name _____

1. Color each thermometer to show the temperature.

September Temperatures

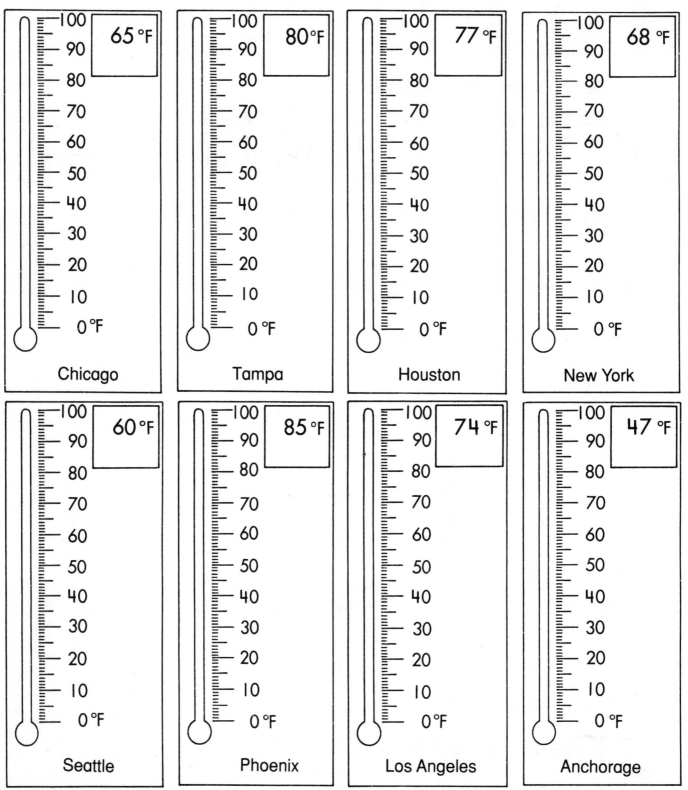

65 °F — Chicago
80 °F — Tampa
77 °F — Houston
68 °F — New York
60 °F — Seattle
85 °F — Phoenix
74 °F — Los Angeles
47 °F — Anchorage

2. Mark the city with the highest temperature.

3. Put a X on the city with the lowest temperature.

Topic 5: Investigating Tens and Ones

Name _____

Which is more? Ring the correct answer.

fifty-four

forty-eight

thirty-nine

thirty-seven

| twenty-five | eighty-one | thirty-seven |
| fifty-two | thirty-nine | thirty-four |

| ninety-eight | seventy-two | seventy-five |
| eighty-nine | seventy-five | fifty-seven |

| sixty-one | twenty-four | forty | seventeen |
| sixteen | twenty-one | twenty | nineteen |

Topic 6: Two-Digit Numbers and Hundreds

Name _____

Number that Came to the Fun Fair

	Mon.	Tue.	Wed.	Thurs.	Fri.	Sat.
Morning	46	62	57	72	89	96
Afternoon	51	58	39	78	98	91

1. For each day, ring the number that is less.

2. Complete these sentences.

Monday

The number was less

in the _____.

_____ is less than _____.

Tuesday

The number was less

in the _____.

_____ is less than _____.

Wednesday

The number was less

in the _____.

_____ is less than _____.

Thursday

_____ is less than _____

Friday

_____ is less than _____

Saturday

_____ is less than _____

3. Write "is less than" or "is greater than."

26 _____ 62

80 _____ 18

56 _____ 52

41 _____ 44

Name _____

1. Color one half of each strip.
   Then ring the number in the middle.

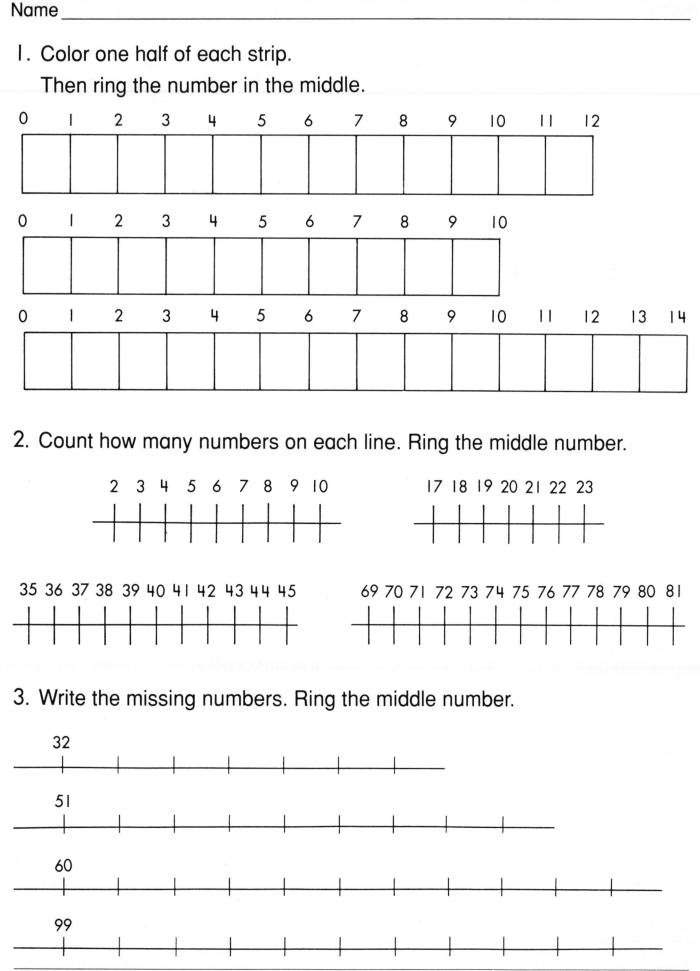

0 1 2 3 4 5 6 7 8 9 10 11 12

0 1 2 3 4 5 6 7 8 9 10

0 1 2 3 4 5 6 7 8 9 10 11 12 13 14

2. Count how many numbers on each line. Ring the middle number.

2 3 4 5 6 7 8 9 10   17 18 19 20 21 22 23

35 36 37 38 39 40 41 42 43 44 45   69 70 71 72 73 74 75 76 77 78 79 80 81

3. Write the missing numbers. Ring the middle number.

32

51

60

99

Name _____

Draw more tens to make one hundred.
Fill in the missing numbers.

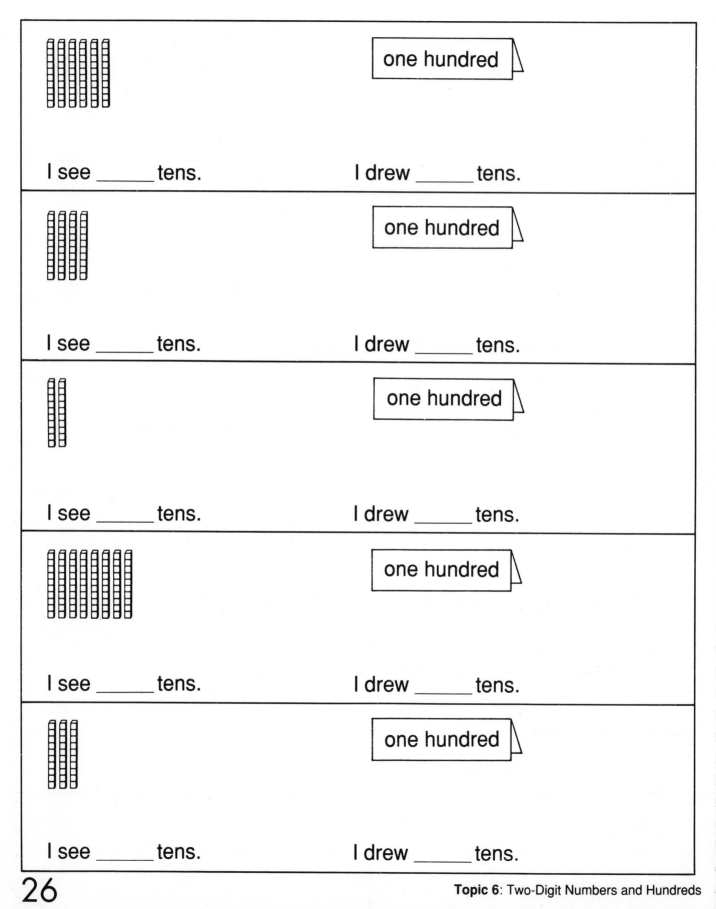

I see _____ tens.   I drew _____ tens.

I see _____ tens.   I drew _____ tens.

I see _____ tens.   I drew _____ tens.

I see _____ tens.   I drew _____ tens.

I see _____ tens.   I drew _____ tens.

Topic 6: Two-Digit Numbers and Hundreds

Name _____

Draw a picture.
Write a number sentence.

Five marbles...
Lose two.

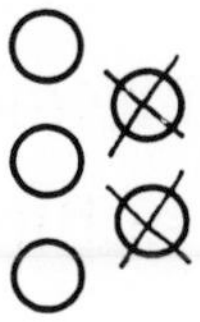

○ ⊗
○ ⊗ 5-2=3
○

Seven marbles . . . lose two.	
Nine birds . . . two fly away.	
Eleven eggs . . . break three.	
Ten dolls . . . give three away.	
Nine toys . . . take four.	
Ten flowers . . . pick one.	

Name _____

Cover one side of each card.

Write a subtraction fact for what you see.

Cover the other side. Write another subtraction fact.

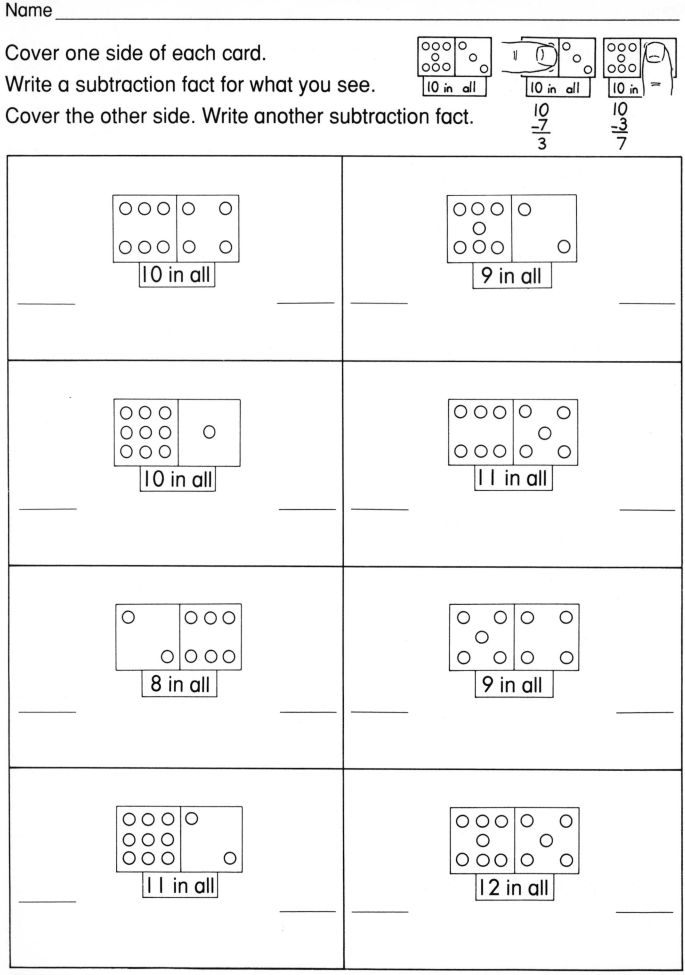

Topic 7: Investigating Subtraction

Name _____

Draw dots on each card to match the addition fact. $\begin{array}{r}8\\ +4\\ \hline 12\end{array}$

Cover one side and then cover the other side.

Write the subtraction facts.

$$\begin{array}{r}12\\ -8\\ \hline 4\end{array} \qquad \begin{array}{r}12\\ -4\\ \hline 8\end{array}$$

$\begin{array}{r}5\\ +2\\ \hline \end{array}$	
$\begin{array}{r}7\\ +4\\ \hline \end{array}$	
$\begin{array}{r}3\\ +9\\ \hline \end{array}$	
$\begin{array}{r}2\\ +8\\ \hline \end{array}$	
$\begin{array}{r}7\\ +1\\ \hline \end{array}$	
$\begin{array}{r}3\\ +8\\ \hline \end{array}$	

Topic 7: Investigating Subtraction

29

Name _____

Write an addition fact and a
subtraction fact for each of these cards.
Then write the answers.

Topic 7: Investigating Subtraction

Name _____

Draw the number in all.   Cover part of the number.

Write an addition sentence and a subtraction sentence.

There are 9 dots. 6 dots on one side. How many dots are on the other side?	9 in all	$6 + 3 = 9$ $9 - 6 = 3$
There are 11 dots. 9 dots on one side. How many dots are on the other side?	11 in all	
There are 10 dots. 7 dots on one side. How many dots on the other side?	10 in all	
I need 8 eggs in all. I have 5 eggs. How many more eggs do I need?	8 in all	
I need 12¢ in all. I have 9¢. How much more do I need?	12 in all	
I want 10 balloons. I have 8 balloons. How many more balloons do I need?	10 in all	

Name _____

1. Write the subtraction fact.

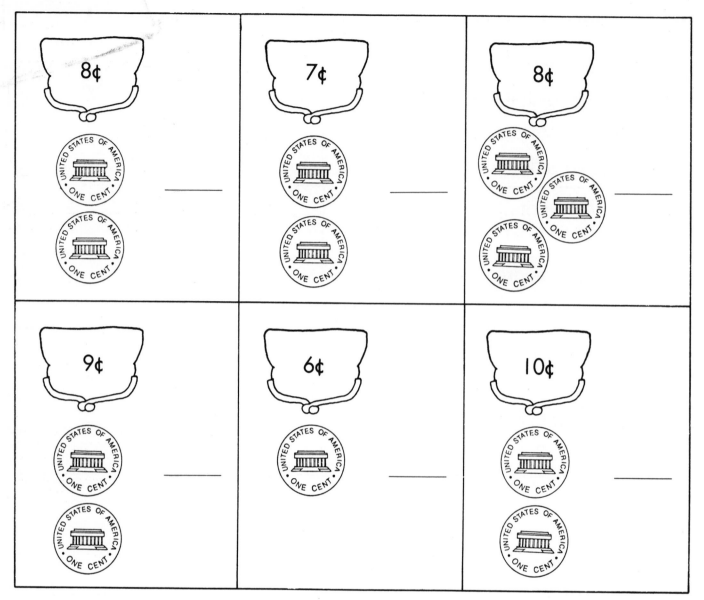

2. Write the answers.

Subtract 2.

8	6	9	7	11
6				

Subtract 3.

7	9	6	11	10

Name _____

1. Draw more dots to help find the answer. Write each answer.

7 − 5	**7 in all**	9 − 6	**9 in all**
6 − 4	**6 in all**	8 − 6	**8 in all**
10 − 7	**10 in all**	11 − 9	**11 in all**
10 − 8	**10 in all**	12 − 9	**12 in all**

2. Write the answers.

7 − 6	7 − 4	7 − 5		9 − 6	9 − 8	9 − 7
10 − 7	10 − 8	10 − 9		8 − 7	8 − 5	8 − 6

Name_____

1. Write the answers as quickly as you can.

6	9	7	8	8	7	9	5	8	11
−1	−2	−3	−3	−2	−2	−1	−2	−1	−3

2. Write what is hidden under each finger.
Write it on the finger.

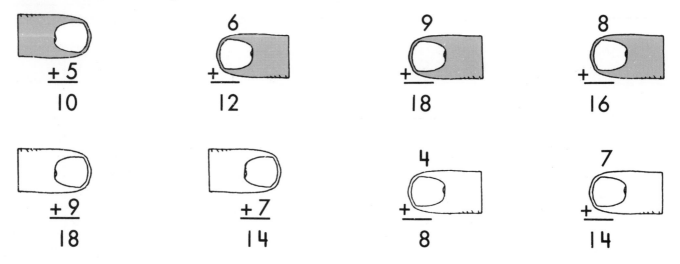

3. Write the missing numbers. Then write a matching subtraction fact.

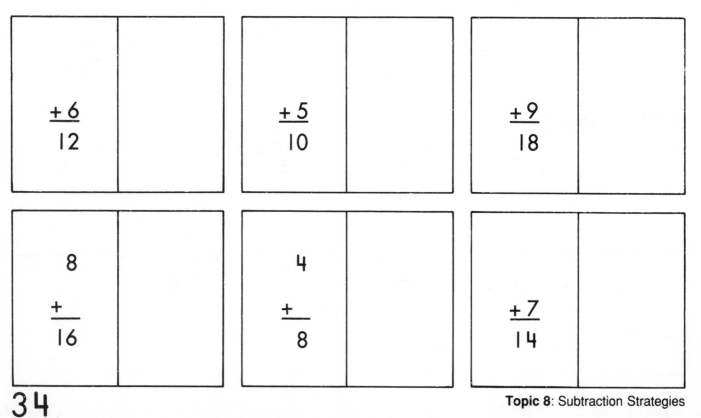

Name _____

Draw dots on each card to match the addition fact.

Cover one side and then cover the other side.

Write subtraction facts for what you see.

$$\begin{array}{r} 0 \\ +3 \\ \hline 3 \end{array} \qquad \begin{array}{r} 3 \\ -0 \\ \hline 3 \end{array} \qquad \begin{array}{r} 3 \\ -3 \\ \hline 0 \end{array}$$

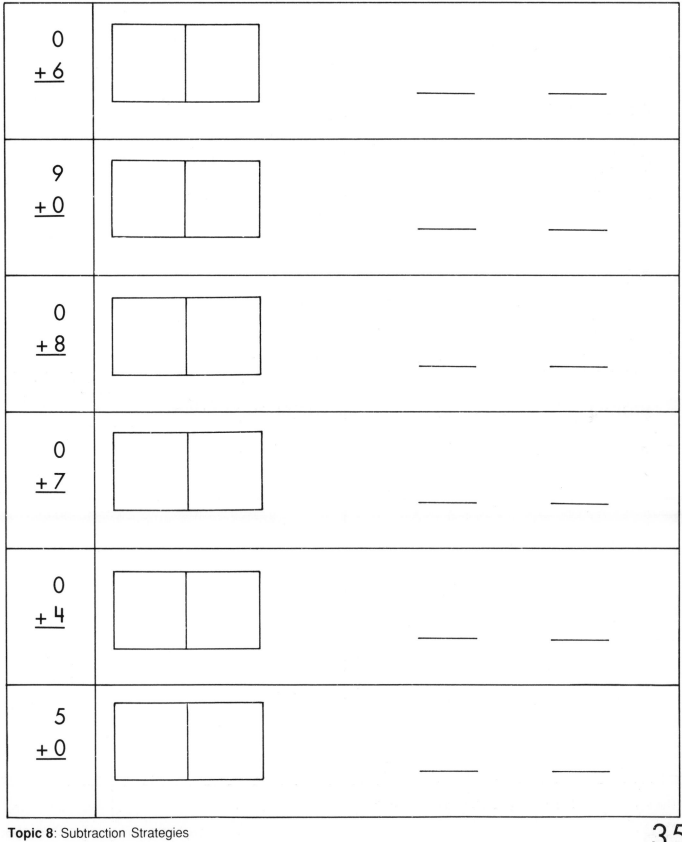

Name _____

Paste word cards to match each shape.
Use solid shapes to help.

I curved face

3 faces

cube 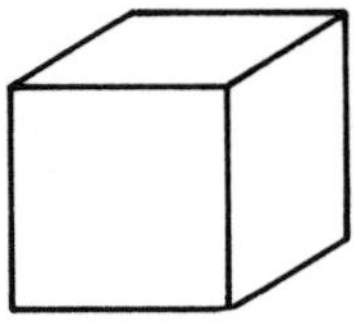	cylinder 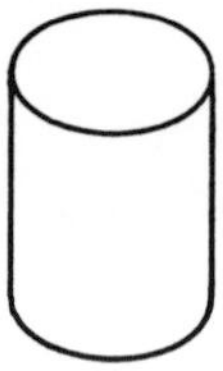
pyramid 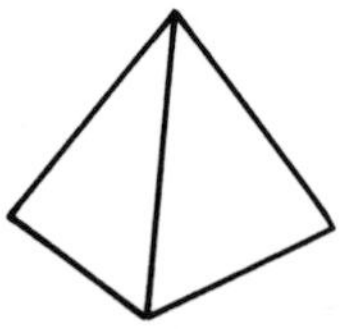	rectangular prism 

The word cards are reproduced on Blackline Master 38.

Topic 9: Investigating Solid Shapes

Name _____

1. Cover each mat with a layer of ones blocks.
Write how many blocks you used.

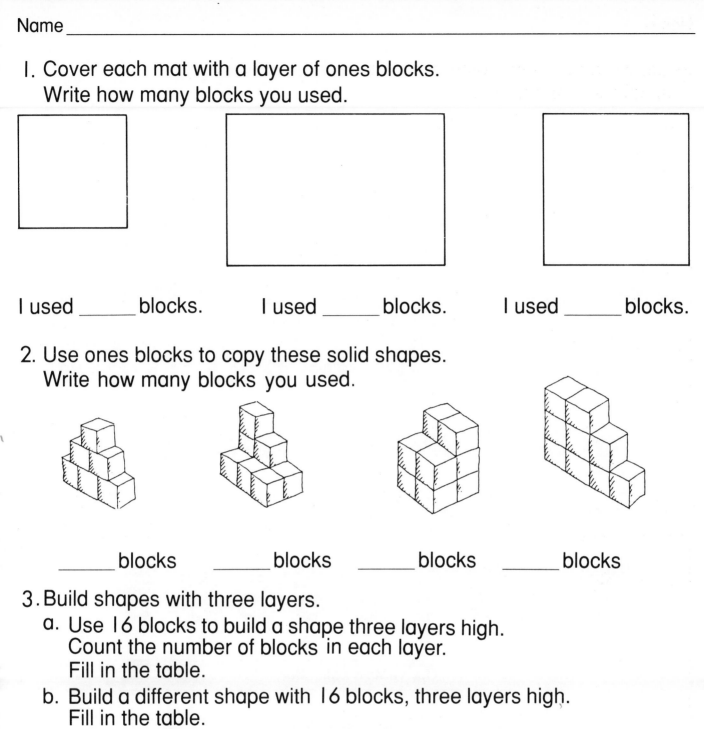

I used _____ blocks.   I used _____ blocks.   I used _____ blocks.

2. Use ones blocks to copy these solid shapes.
Write how many blocks you used.

_____ blocks   _____ blocks   _____ blocks   _____ blocks

3. Build shapes with three layers.
   a. Use 16 blocks to build a shape three layers high.
      Count the number of blocks in each layer.
      Fill in the table.

   b. Build a different shape with 16 blocks, three layers high.
      Fill in the table.

Building three layers		
	1st shape	2nd shape
top layer	blocks	blocks
middle layer	blocks	blocks
bottom layer (base)	blocks	blocks

Name _____

Color these so all the same kind are the same color.
Use the same colors to fill in the graph.

Our vehicle collection														
dump trucks														
ambulances														
racing cars														
fire engines														
cement mixers														
		I	2	3	4	5	6	7	8	9	I0	II	I2

Check the row with the most.
Put a X on the row with the least.

Topic 10: Visual Representation - graphing

Name _____

1. You will need five large containers and a one-liter container.
   Write the name of each container on the graph.

2. Color in the graph to show about how many liters of water
   each container holds. *Estimate before you measure.*

Containers	Number of liters each container holds
 two-liter container	

Number of liters   1   2   3   4   5   6   7   8   9   10   11   12   13   14   15   16

3. Which container holds the most? _____

4. Which container holds the least? _____

5. Make up two questions about the graph. _____

_____

_____

_____

> *Example*
> How much more
> does the pail
> hold than the
> pan?

Name _____

Some children measured their classroom.

	Meters
front wall (length)	7
side wall (length)	8
windows (width)	2
door (height)	2
chalkboard (width)	3
table (length)	1

1. Show the classroom measurements on the graph.
2. Write a title on the graph.

10 meters

9 meters

8 meters

7 meters

6 meters

5 meters

4 meters

3 meters

2 meters

1 meter

front wall   side wall   windows   door   chalkboard   table

3. Use the graph to complete these sentences.

The _____ is the longest measurement.

The _____ and the _____ measure the same.

The difference between the lengths of the two walls is

_____ meter.

Measure some things in your classroom. Show them on the graph.

Name _____

Draw more blocks to
fill in each grid.
Then write two addition facts.

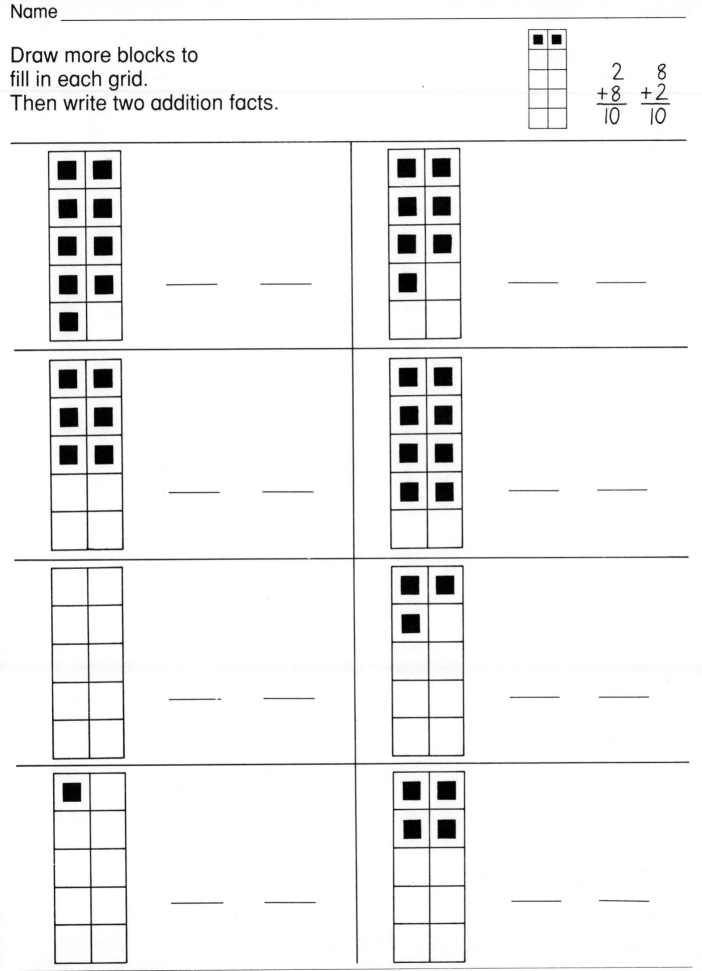

$$\begin{array}{cc} 2 & 8 \\ +8 & +2 \\ \hline 10 & 10 \end{array}$$

Name _____

Draw more blocks to
fill in each grid.
Then write two addition facts.

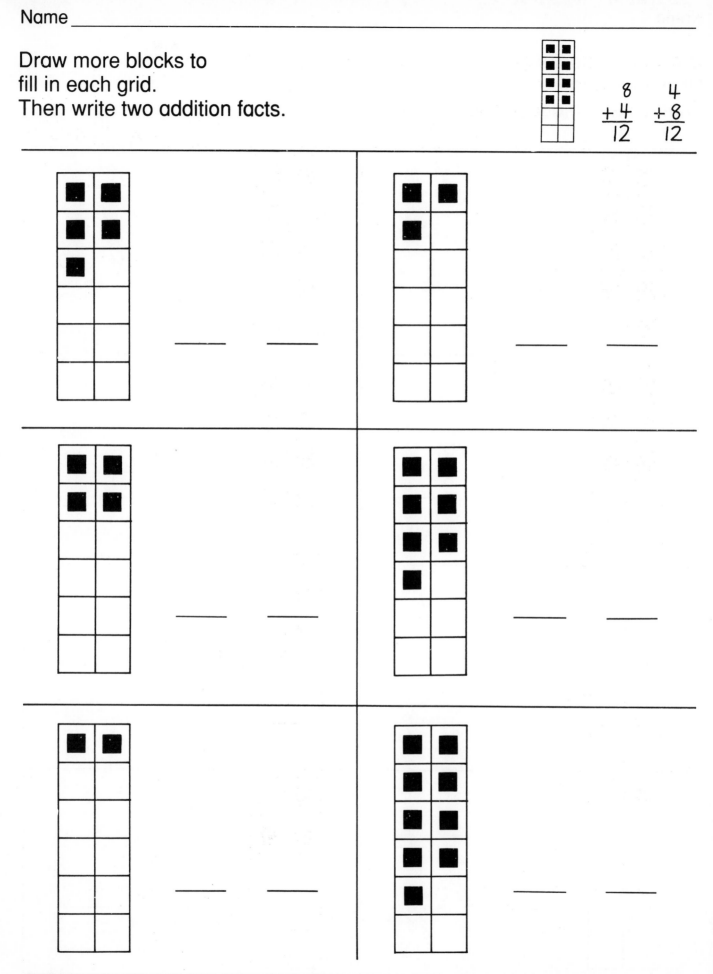

$$\begin{array}{r} 8 \\ +4 \\ \hline 12 \end{array} \qquad \begin{array}{r} 4 \\ +8 \\ \hline 12 \end{array}$$

Name _____

Color just enough beads to show the top number in each fact.
Use a different color to show the bottom number.
Then ring ten beads and write the answer.

$$\begin{array}{r} 9 \\ +3 \\ \hline 12 \end{array}$$

⬤⬤⬤⬤⬤⬤⬤⬤⬤◍
◍◍○○○○○○○○

$\begin{array}{r} 9 \\ +8 \\ \hline \end{array}$ ○○○○○○○○○○ ○○○○○○○○○○	$\begin{array}{r} 9 \\ +6 \\ \hline \end{array}$ ○○○○○○○○○○ ○○○○○○○○○○
$\begin{array}{r} 9 \\ +4 \\ \hline \end{array}$ ○○○○○○○○○○ ○○○○○○○○○○	$\begin{array}{r} 8 \\ +5 \\ \hline \end{array}$ ○○○○○○○○○○ ○○○○○○○○○○
$\begin{array}{r} 9 \\ +5 \\ \hline \end{array}$ ○○○○○○○○○○ ○○○○○○○○○○	$\begin{array}{r} 9 \\ +7 \\ \hline \end{array}$ ○○○○○○○○○○ ○○○○○○○○○○
$\begin{array}{r} 8 \\ +4 \\ \hline \end{array}$ ○○○○○○○○○○ ○○○○○○○○○○	$\begin{array}{r} 8 \\ +6 \\ \hline \end{array}$ ○○○○○○○○○○ ○○○○○○○○○○

Topic 11: Addition Strategies – using tens

43

Name _____

Add the numbers in the ones column.
Check to see if you can make a ten.
Then add the numbers in the tens column.

tens	ones		tens	ones		tens	ones		tens	ones
5	6		3	2		1	4		1	3
+ 3	1		+ 3	5		+ 5	4		+ 1	6

```
   6 7        4 1        2 3        6 5
 + 3 2      + 5 8      + 5 3      + 2 4
```

```
   3 1        2 4        6 7        1 5
 + 2 6      + 1 4      + 1 2      + 6 1
```

```
   1 3        2 4        3 1        5 8
 + 7 3      + 2 5      + 4 1      + 2 1
```

```
   5 5        7 8        5 2        3 6
 + 3 4      + 1 1      +   7      + 2 0
```

44

32¢   40¢   25¢

41¢   43¢   52¢

1. Use dimes and pennies to help answer these.

Buy [mug]

and [mouse] $\begin{array}{r} 32 \\ +52 \\ \hline 84 \end{array}$

How much do you pay?

I pay 84¢.

How much do you

pay for [maze]

and [mug] ?   _____

What will it cost

to buy [glasses]

and [comb] ?   _____

Sue buys [star]

and [glasses]

What does she pay?   _____

How much do the

[comb] and [mug] cost?   _____

What would you pay for

[comb] and [star] ?   _____

2. Try these questions.

What will [mug]

[comb] and [glasses] cost?   _____

Buy [mug] [star] and [comb]

What will they cost?   _____

_____

Topic 12: Exploring Addition of Two-Digit Numbers

45

Name _____

1. Put 10 tens blocks on a pan balance.
   Find out how many of each pattern
   block you need to balance them.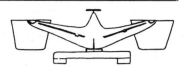

2. Color the graph to show what you found out.

3. Write a title for the graph.

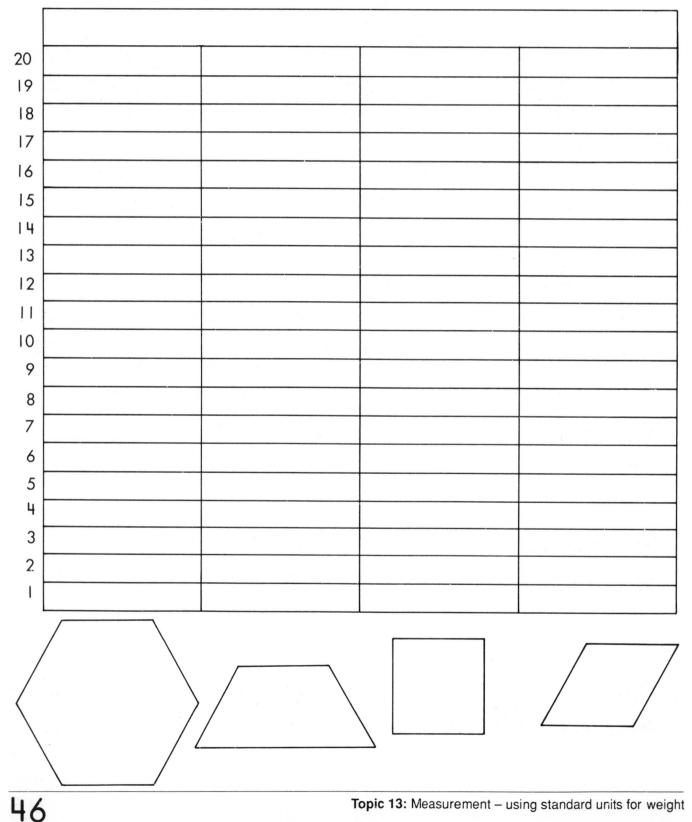

Topic 13: Measurement – using standard units for weight

Name _____

Balance these objects against a kilogram weight.
Write your results in the table below.

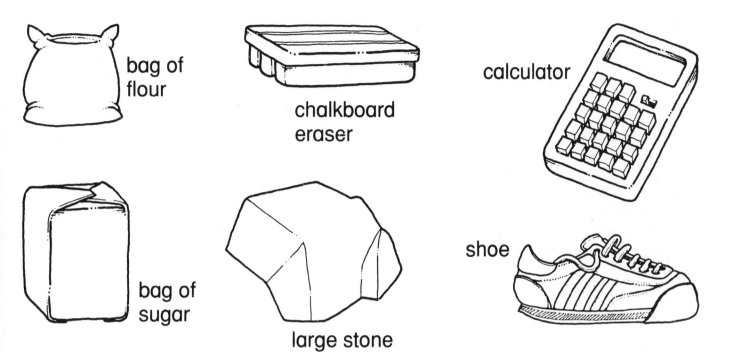

bag of flour

chalkboard eraser

calculator

bag of sugar

large stone

shoe

Objects	More than one kilogram	Equal to one kilogram	Less than one kilogram
shoe			
flour			
chalkboard eraser			
large stone			
sugar			
calculator			

Name _____

1. Use two colors to color these hexagons.

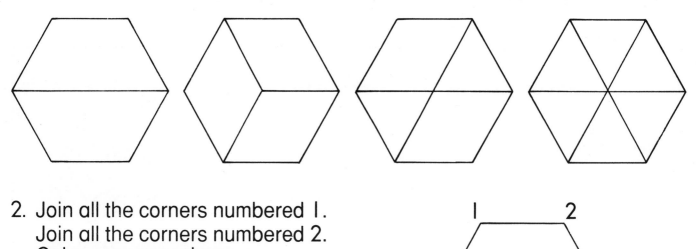

2. Join all the corners numbered 1.
   Join all the corners numbered 2.
   Color your new shape.
   What shape did you draw?

   _____

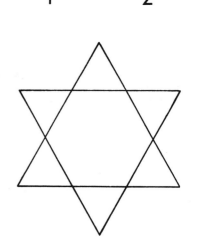

3. Join the six points
   of the star.
   Color a new pattern.
   What shape did you draw?

   _____

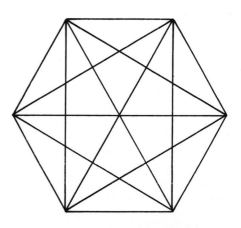

4. Color the shapes in this
   hexagon to make a pattern.

Topic 14: Introducing More Plane Shapes

Name _____

1. Draw lines to join each set of dots in order.
   Join the last dot to the first dot to make a closed shape.

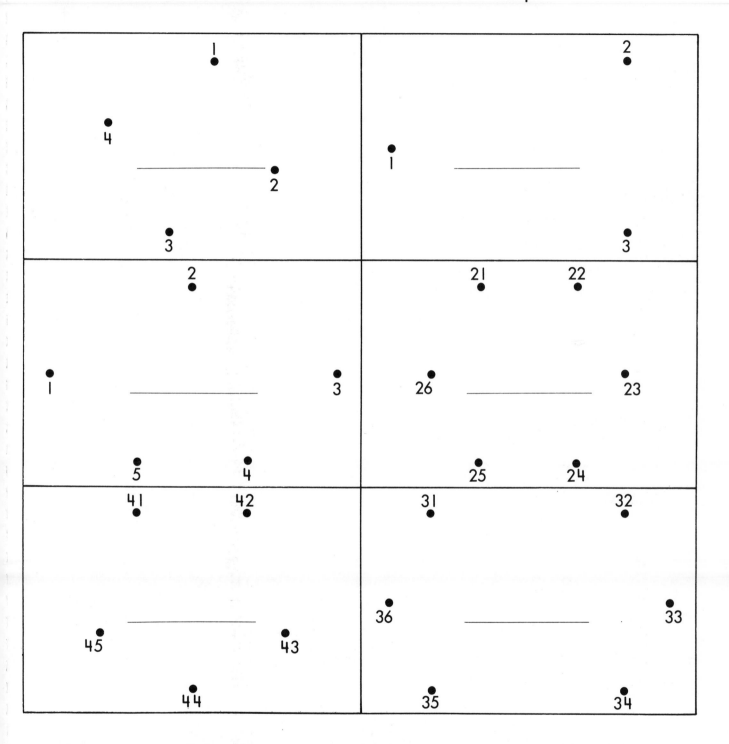

2. Choose the correct name to write inside each shape you made.
   You may use the same name twice.

| hexagon | pentagon | triangle | square |

Topic 14: Introducing More Plane Shapes

Name _____

Draw dots on each card to make the number in all.
Write the numbers.

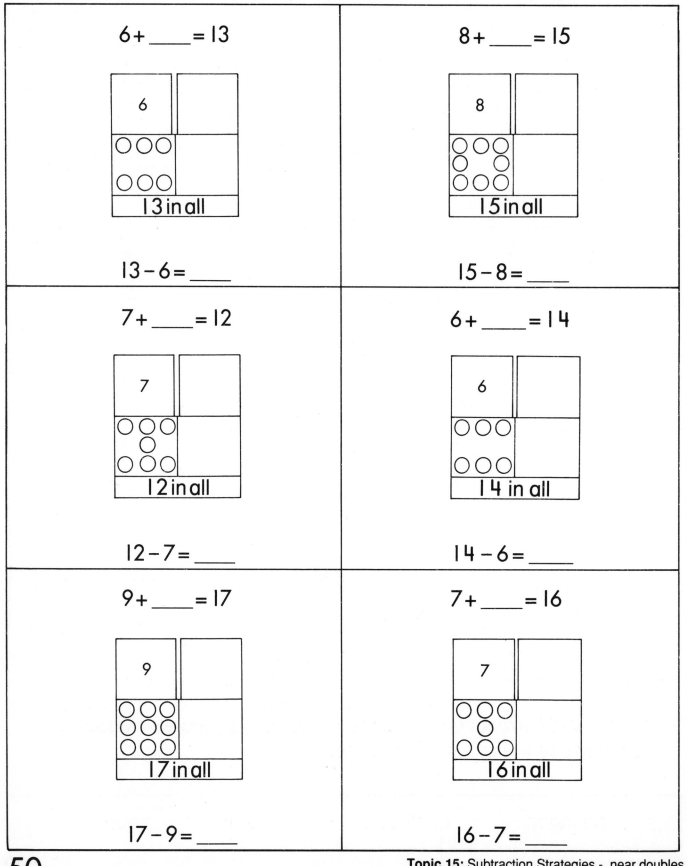

$6 + \underline{\hspace{1cm}} = 13$

6

13 in all

$13 - 6 = \underline{\hspace{1cm}}$

$8 + \underline{\hspace{1cm}} = 15$

8

15 in all

$15 - 8 = \underline{\hspace{1cm}}$

$7 + \underline{\hspace{1cm}} = 12$

7

12 in all

$12 - 7 = \underline{\hspace{1cm}}$

$6 + \underline{\hspace{1cm}} = 14$

6

14 in all

$14 - 6 = \underline{\hspace{1cm}}$

$9 + \underline{\hspace{1cm}} = 17$

9

17 in all

$17 - 9 = \underline{\hspace{1cm}}$

$7 + \underline{\hspace{1cm}} = 16$

7

16 in all

$16 - 7 = \underline{\hspace{1cm}}$

Topic 15: Subtraction Strategies - near doubles

Name _____

Draw dots on each card to make the number in all.
Write an addition and a subtraction fact.

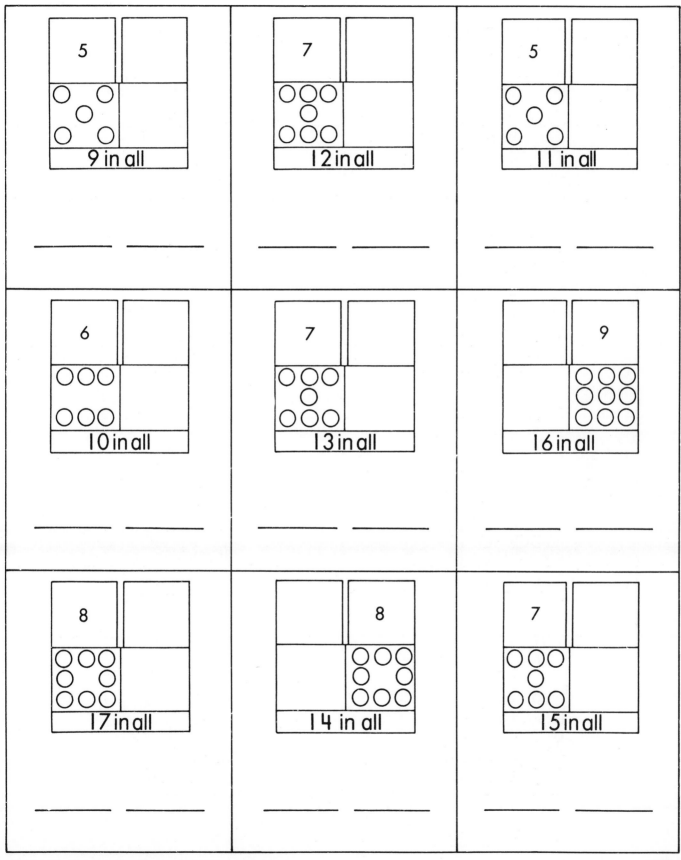

Name _____

For each card, write two addition facts and two subtraction facts.

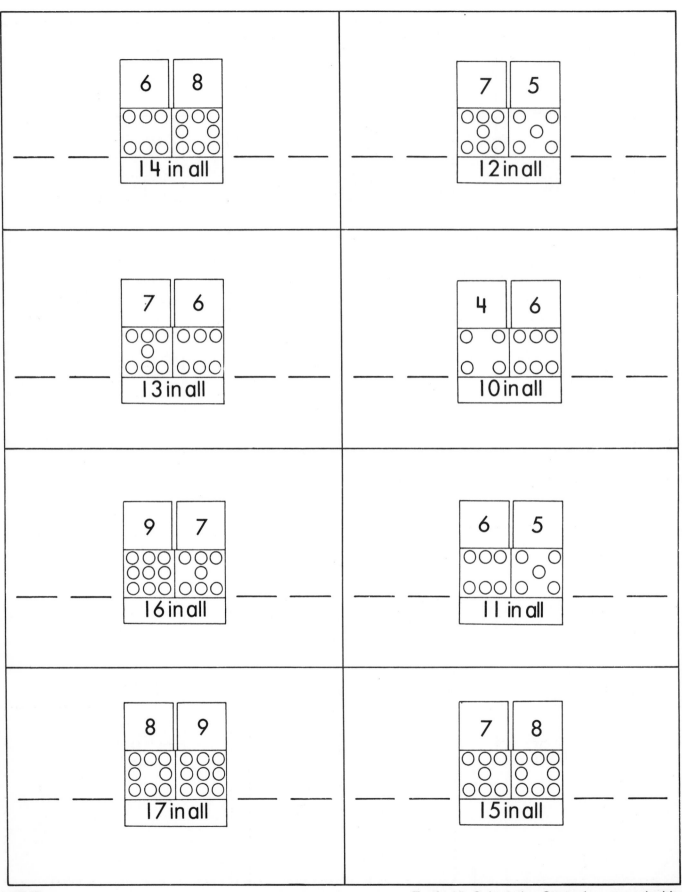

Topic 15: Subtraction Strategies - near doubles

Name _____

1. Write the answer for each addition fact.
2. Write two subtraction facts for each.

$$\begin{array}{r} 3 \\ +5 \\ \hline 8 \end{array}\quad\begin{array}{r} 8 \\ -5 \\ \hline 3 \end{array}\quad\begin{array}{r} 8 \\ -3 \\ \hline 5 \end{array}$$

$\begin{array}{r}5\\+6\\\hline\end{array}$	___ ___	$\begin{array}{r}4\\+5\\\hline\end{array}$	___ ___
$\begin{array}{r}7\\+5\\\hline\end{array}$	___ ___	$\begin{array}{r}6\\+5\\\hline\end{array}$	___ ___
$\begin{array}{r}6\\+7\\\hline\end{array}$	___ ___	$\begin{array}{r}8\\+6\\\hline\end{array}$	___ ___
$\begin{array}{r}6\\+4\\\hline\end{array}$	___ ___	$\begin{array}{r}7\\+9\\\hline\end{array}$	___ ___
$\begin{array}{r}9\\+8\\\hline\end{array}$	___ ___	$\begin{array}{r}8\\+7\\\hline\end{array}$	___ ___

Topic 15: Subtraction Strategies - near doubles

53

Name _____

1. Write the answer for each addition fact.

2. Write two subtraction facts for each.

$$\begin{array}{r} 3 \\ +4 \\ \hline 7 \end{array} \quad \begin{array}{r} 7 \\ -3 \\ \hline 4 \end{array} \quad \begin{array}{r} 7 \\ -4 \\ \hline 3 \end{array}$$

$\begin{array}{r} 7 \\ +6 \\ \hline \end{array}$ ___ ___	$\begin{array}{r} 5 \\ +4 \\ \hline \end{array}$ ___ ___
$\begin{array}{r} 8 \\ +7 \\ \hline \end{array}$ ___ ___	$\begin{array}{r} 6 \\ +5 \\ \hline \end{array}$ ___ ___
$\begin{array}{r} 9 \\ +8 \\ \hline \end{array}$ ___ ___	$\begin{array}{r} 7 \\ +8 \\ \hline \end{array}$ ___ ___
$\begin{array}{r} 6 \\ +7 \\ \hline \end{array}$ ___ ___	$\begin{array}{r} 8 \\ +9 \\ \hline \end{array}$ ___ ___

3. Write the answers.

$$\begin{array}{r} 9 \\ -4 \\ \hline \end{array} \qquad \begin{array}{r} 11 \\ -6 \\ \hline \end{array} \qquad \begin{array}{r} 7 \\ -3 \\ \hline \end{array} \qquad \begin{array}{r} 9 \\ -5 \\ \hline \end{array} \qquad \begin{array}{r} 11 \\ -5 \\ \hline \end{array} \qquad \begin{array}{r} 7 \\ -4 \\ \hline \end{array}$$

$$\begin{array}{r} 15 \\ -7 \\ \hline \end{array} \qquad \begin{array}{r} 17 \\ -8 \\ \hline \end{array} \qquad \begin{array}{r} 13 \\ -6 \\ \hline \end{array} \qquad \begin{array}{r} 15 \\ -8 \\ \hline \end{array} \qquad \begin{array}{r} 13 \\ -7 \\ \hline \end{array} \qquad \begin{array}{r} 17 \\ -9 \\ \hline \end{array}$$

Topic 15: Subtraction Strategies - near doubles

Follow these three steps to subtract.

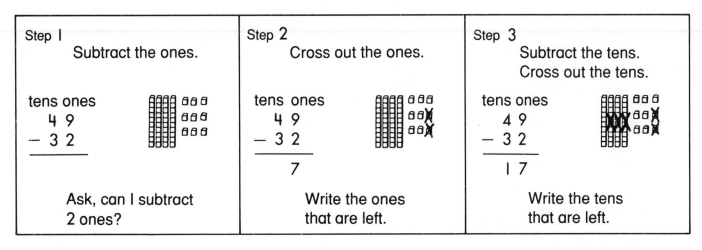

Step 1	Step 2	Step 3
Subtract the ones.	Cross out the ones.	Subtract the tens. Cross out the tens.

tens ones
  4 9
− 3 2
_____
	tens ones
	  4 9
	− 3 2
	_____
	      7
		tens ones
		  4 9
		− 3 2
		_____
		   1 7

Ask, can I subtract 2 ones?	Write the ones that are left.	Write the tens that are left.

Use the three steps to answer these.

tens ones
  6 7
− 3 2
_____

tens ones
  8 9
− 4 1
_____

tens ones
  7 5
− 2 1
_____

tens ones
  5 6
− 3 2
_____

tens ones
  9 8
− 3 4
_____

tens ones
  6 4
− 5 2
_____

Topic 16: Exploring Subtraction of Two-Digit Numbers

Name _____

1. Draw a line to join each story to the correct box.

2. Use dimes and pennies to help figure out the answers.

3. Write the answers.

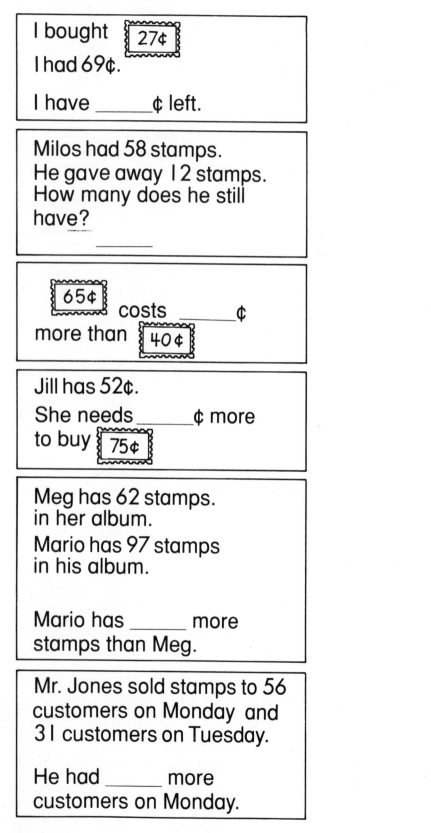

I bought 27¢
I had 69¢.

I have _____ ¢ left.

Milos had 58 stamps.
He gave away 12 stamps.
How many does he still
have?

_____

65¢ costs _____ ¢
more than 40¢

Jill has 52¢.
She needs _____ ¢ more
to buy 75¢

Meg has 62 stamps.
in her album.
Mario has 97 stamps
in his album.

Mario has _____ more
stamps than Meg.

Mr. Jones sold stamps to 56
customers on Monday and
31 customers on Tuesday.

He had _____ more
customers on Monday.

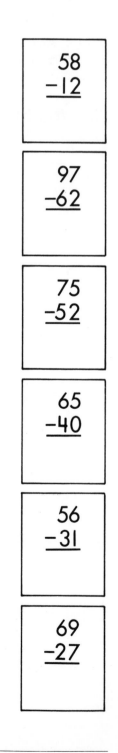

$$\begin{array}{r}58\\-12\\\hline\end{array}$$

$$\begin{array}{r}97\\-62\\\hline\end{array}$$

$$\begin{array}{r}75\\-52\\\hline\end{array}$$

$$\begin{array}{r}65\\-40\\\hline\end{array}$$

$$\begin{array}{r}56\\-31\\\hline\end{array}$$

$$\begin{array}{r}69\\-27\\\hline\end{array}$$

56

Name _____

1. Write how many more ones are needed to make the next ten.

53	21	17	92	40	34	6	49	68
7								

2. Ring ones to make a ten, if you can.
   Then ring tens to make a hundred, if you can.
   Write the numbers after you have traded.

_____ hundreds _____ tens _____ ones   _____ hundreds _____ tens _____ ones

_____ hundreds _____ tens _____ ones   _____ hundreds _____ tens _____ ones

_____ hundreds _____ tens _____ ones   _____ hundreds _____ tens _____ ones

3. Show these with blocks. Trade tens for hundreds.
   Write how many hundreds and tens you have then.

26 tens	48 tens
_____ hundreds _____ tens	_____ hundreds _____ tens
17 tens	30 tens
_____ hundreds _____ tens	_____ hundreds _____ tens

Topic 17: Hundreds, Tens, and Ones

57

Name _____

Write how many hundreds, tens, and ones you see.
Then write the number in words.

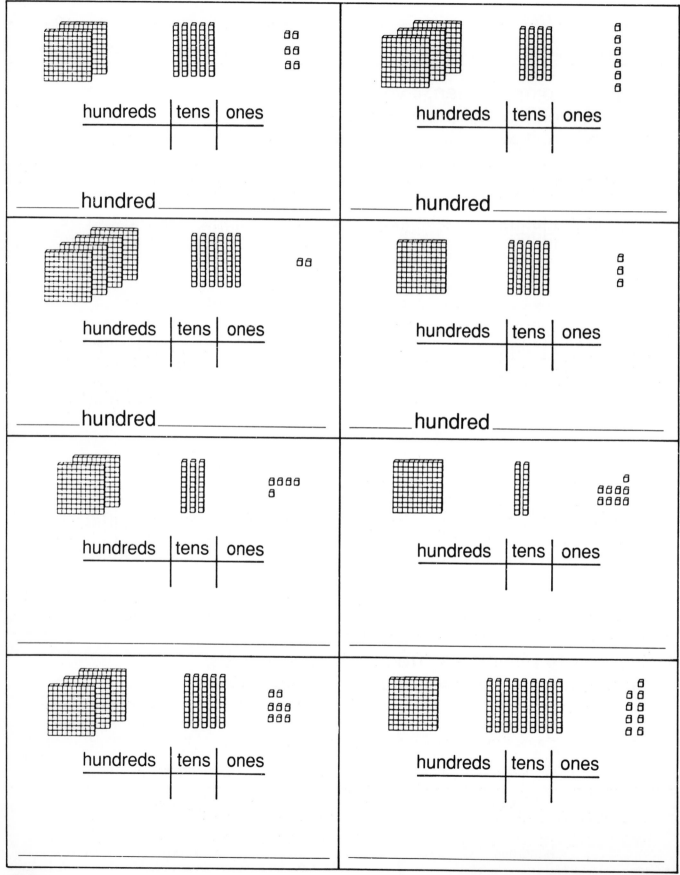

hundreds	tens	ones

_____ hundred _____

hundreds	tens	ones

_____ hundred _____

hundreds	tens	ones

_____ hundred _____

hundreds	tens	ones

_____ hundred _____

hundreds	tens	ones

hundreds	tens	ones

hundreds	tens	ones

hundreds	tens	ones

58

Name _____

1. Show each number with pictures of blocks.
   Then fill in the number expander.

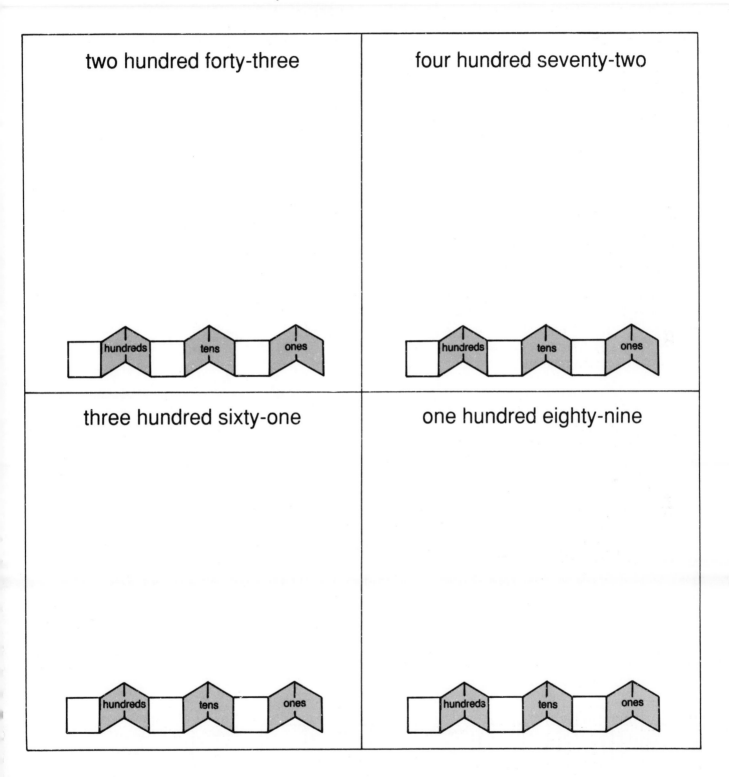

two hundred forty-three	four hundred seventy-two
hundreds tens ones	hundreds tens ones
three hundred sixty-one	one hundred eighty-nine
hundreds tens ones	hundreds tens ones

2. Write each of these on an expander.

five hundred ninety-four   one hundred sixty-five
two hundred thirty-nine   three hundred twenty-one

Name _____

1. Write the number of hundreds, tens, and ones on the open expander.
2. Write the number in words.
3. Write the number on the closed expander.

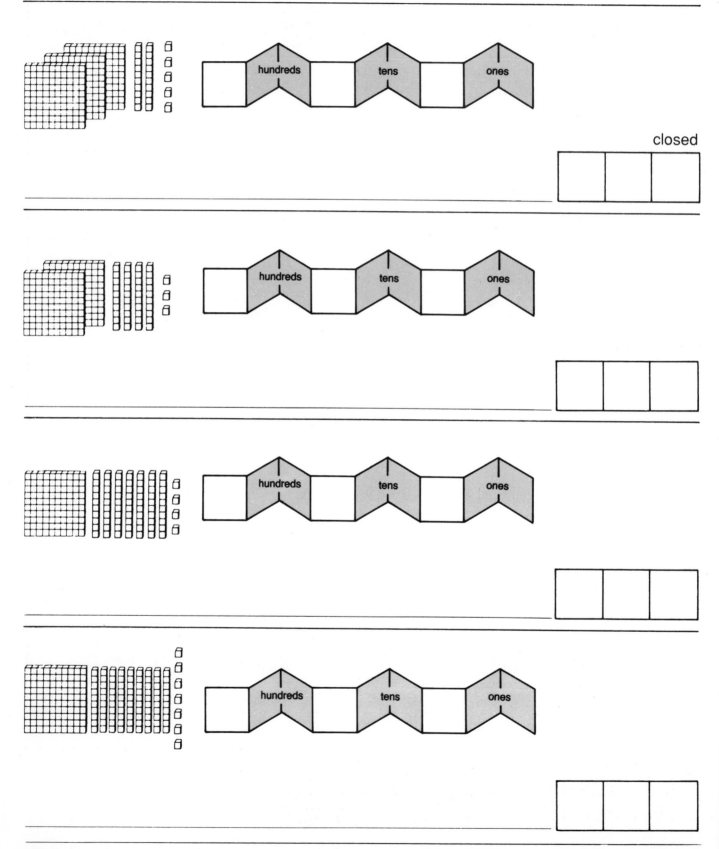

Name _____

1. Show each number with pictures of blocks.
   Write each number in words.

245 _____ _____	357 _____ _____
284 _____ _____	46 _____ _____
428 _____ _____	84 _____ _____

2. Check the four that is in the hundreds place.
   Ring all the fours that are in the tens place.
   Underline all the fours that are in the ones place.

Name_____

1. Put a X on the digit in the ones place.
   Ring the digit in the tens place.

   92   276   80   16   380   400

2. Write the number of hundreds, tens, and ones on the open expander.

3. Write the number word.

4. Write the number on the closed expander.

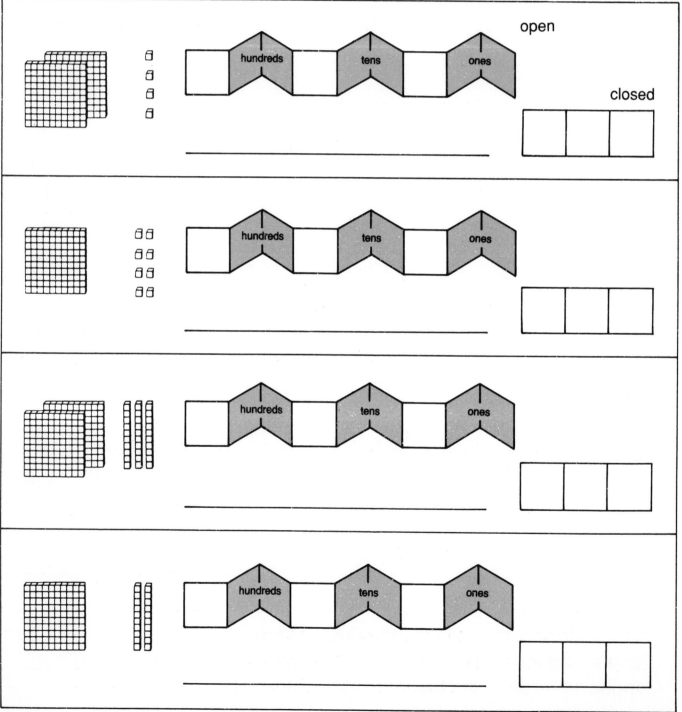

Topic 18: Place Value with Three-Digit Numbers

Name _____

1. Write the number on the closed expander.
   Write the number in words.

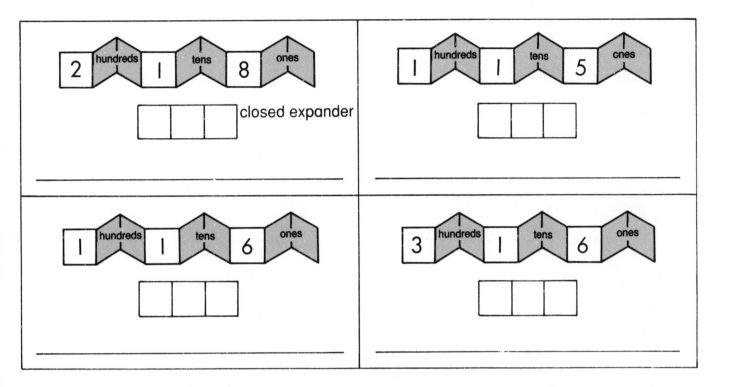

closed expander

2. Write the number on the open expander.
   Write the number in words.

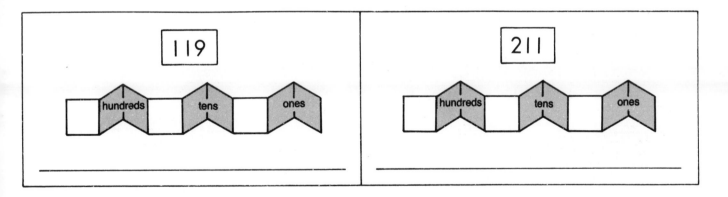

3. Write each number.

one hundred twelve _____	one hundred seventy _____
two hundred fourteen _____	one hundred seventeen _____

Name _____

1. Ring the number that is less in each pair.
   Write the numbers on the labels.
   Complete the sentence.

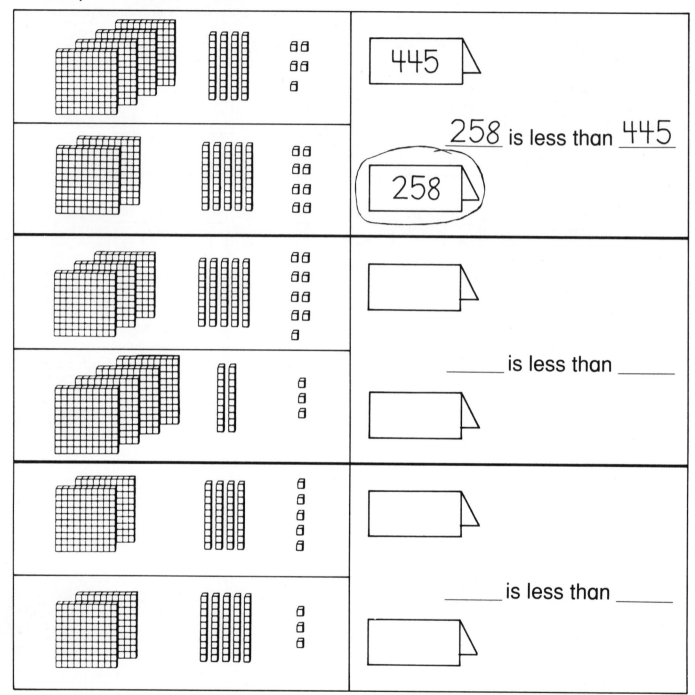

258 is less than 445

_____ is less than _____

_____ is less than _____

2. Ring the greatest number.

624	341	129	236
599	431	135	362
129	295	187	326

Topic 18: Place Value with Three-Digit Numbers

Name _____

1. In each picture, ring coins to make one quarter.

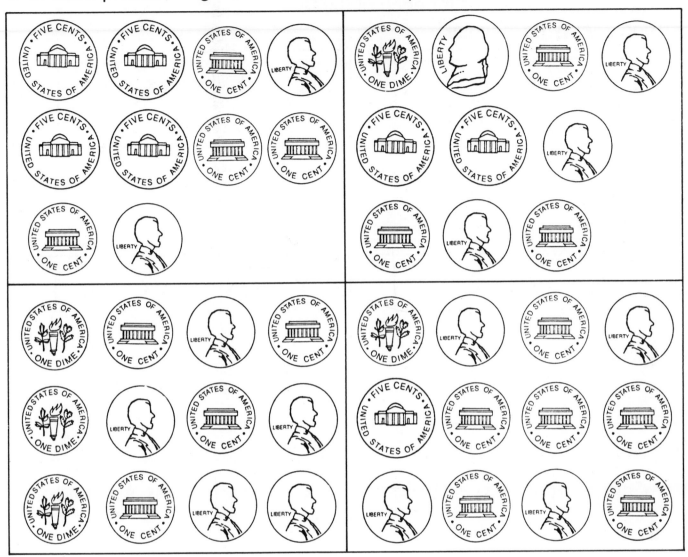

2. Write the amount of money.

_____ ¢

_____ ¢

_____ ¢

_____ ¢

Name _____

1. Draw pictures of coins for each of these.
   Ring 25¢. Write the total.

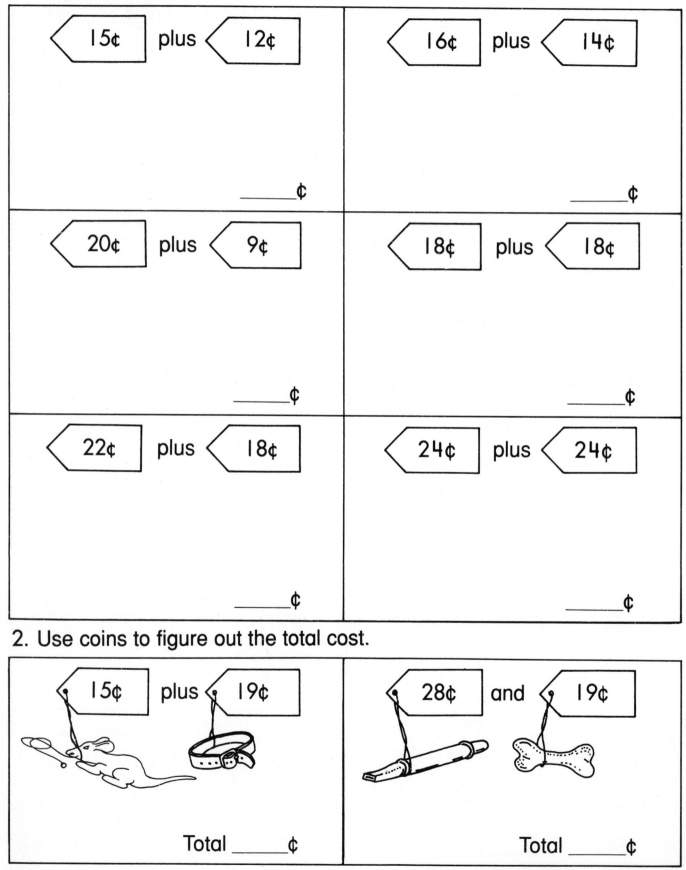

15¢ plus 12¢ _____¢	16¢ plus 14¢ _____¢
20¢ plus 9¢ _____¢	18¢ plus 18¢ _____¢
22¢ plus 18¢ _____¢	24¢ plus 24¢ _____¢

2. Use coins to figure out the total cost.

15¢ plus 19¢ Total _____¢	28¢ and 19¢ Total _____¢

Topic 19: Money - using new coins

1. Cross out enough coins to match the amount on the price tag.
   Write the amount that is left.

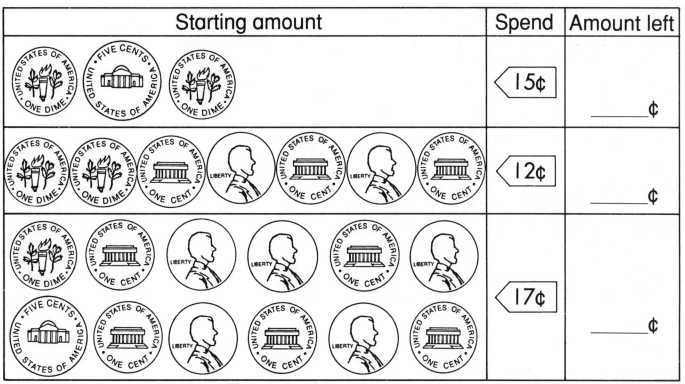

Starting amount	Spend	Amount left
(dime, nickel, dime)	15¢	_____ ¢
(dime, dime, penny, penny, penny, penny, penny)	12¢	_____ ¢
(dime, penny, penny, penny, penny, penny, nickel, penny, penny, penny, penny, penny, penny)	17¢	_____ ¢

2. Draw coins to show 25¢. Use three different ways.
   Cross out enough coins to match the amount on the price tag.
   Write the amount that is left.

Starting amount 25¢	Spend	Amount left
	10¢	_____ ¢
	9 ¢	_____ ¢
	14¢	_____ ¢

3. Start with one quarter. Trade for other coins. Write the amount left.

| Start with one quarter. | Spend | 16¢ | _____ ¢ is left. |
| Start with one quarter. | Spend | 7¢ | _____ ¢ is left. |

Topic 19: Money - using new coins

Name _____

1. Ring 50¢ in each picture. Write the total.

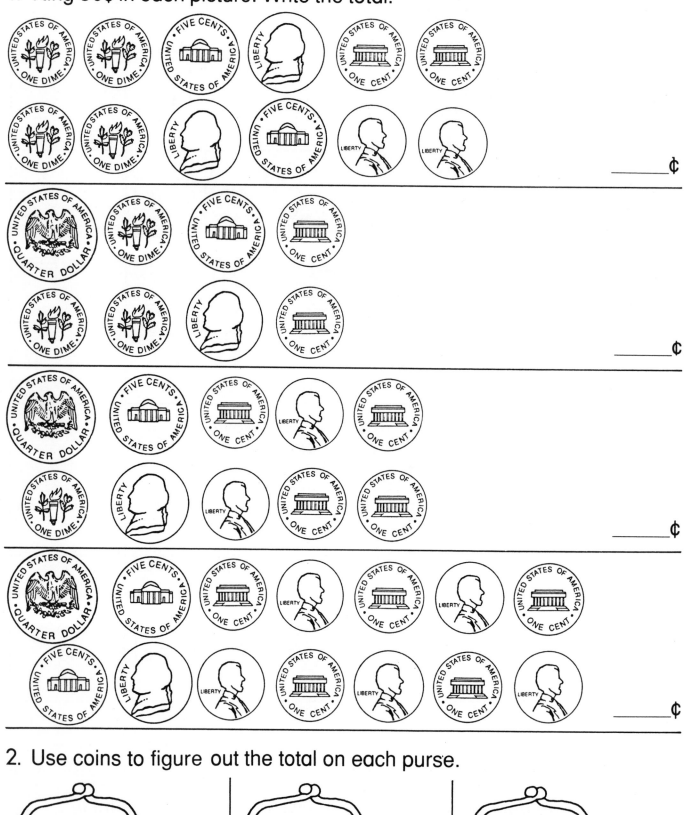

_____ ¢

_____ ¢

_____ ¢

_____ ¢

2. Use coins to figure out the total on each purse.

1 half dollar
1 dime
1 nickel

_____ ¢

1 half dollar
1 quarter
2 dimes

_____ ¢

1 half dollar
3 dimes
4 pennies

_____ ¢

Topic 19: Money - using new coins

Name _____

1. Draw a picture of coins to match each number example.
   Write the total.

$$\begin{array}{r} 52 \\ + 37 \\ \hline \end{array}$$

I drew _____ ¢

$$\begin{array}{r} 61 \\ + 15 \\ \hline \end{array}$$

I drew _____ ¢

$$\begin{array}{r} 45 \\ + 26 \\ \hline \end{array}$$

I drew _____ ¢

$$\begin{array}{r} 18 \\ + 78 \\ \hline \end{array}$$

I drew _____ ¢

2. Write each total. Use coins to help.

$$\begin{array}{r} 32 \\ + 25 \\ \hline \end{array} \qquad \begin{array}{r} 28 \\ + 31 \\ \hline \end{array} \qquad \begin{array}{r} 52 \\ + 16 \\ \hline \end{array} \qquad \begin{array}{r} 39 \\ + 12 \\ \hline \end{array} \qquad \begin{array}{r} 56 \\ + 26 \\ \hline \end{array} \qquad \begin{array}{r} 25 \\ + 45 \\ \hline \end{array}$$

Name _____

1. Draw more coins to make 50¢.

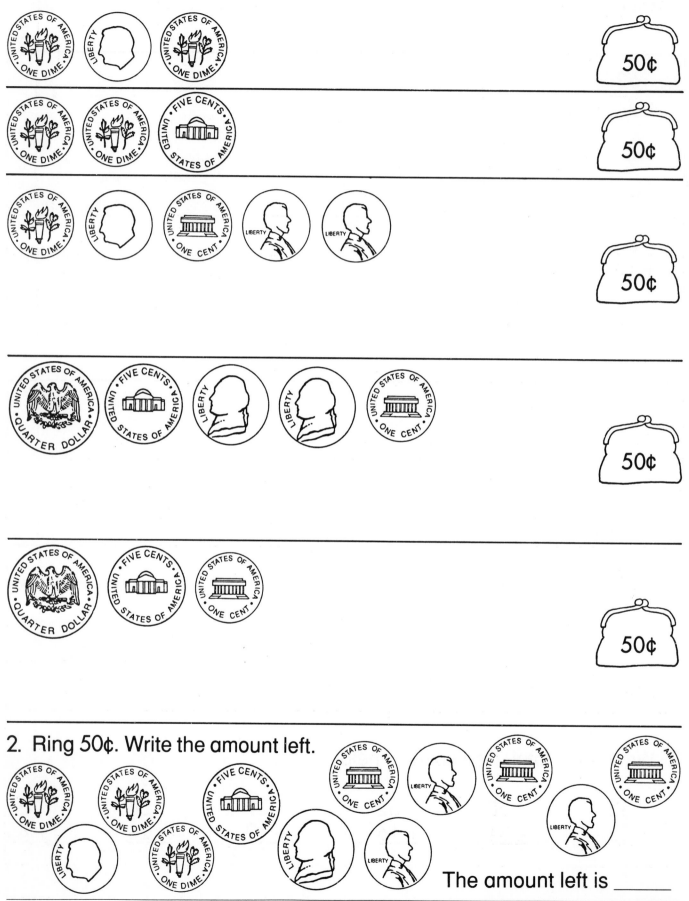

2. Ring 50¢. Write the amount left.

The amount left is _____

Topic 19: Money - using new coins

Name _____

Draw a picture to show each number sentence.
Write how many in all.

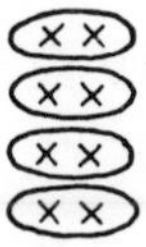

4 sets of 2 is 8

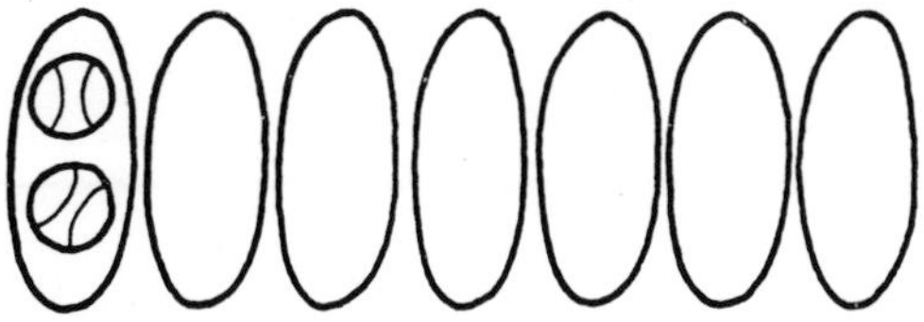

7 sets of 2 is _____

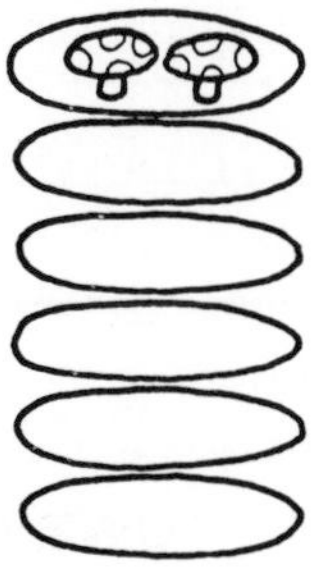

6 groups of 2 is _____

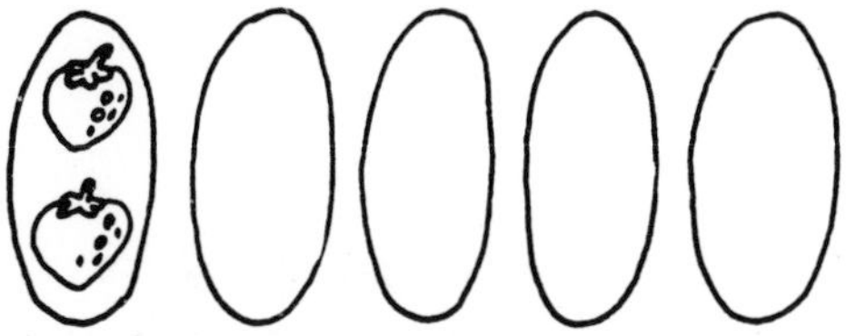

5 bunches of 2 is _____

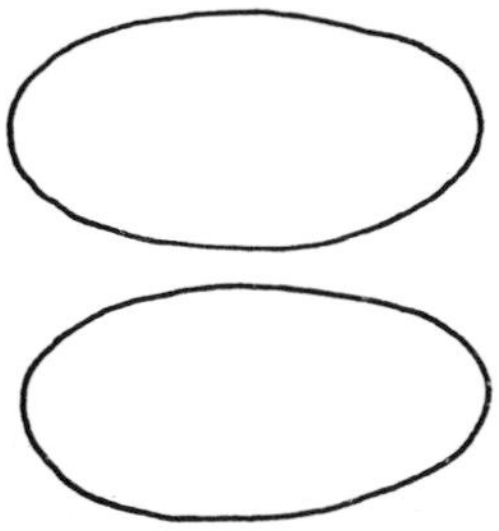

2 sets of 8 is _____

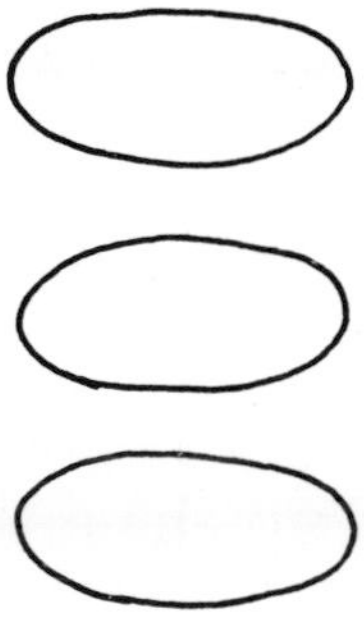

3 groups of 4 is _____

2 bunches of 5 is _____

3 boxes of 5 is _____

5 bags of 3 is _____

Name _____

Shade each row a different color.
Write the numbers.

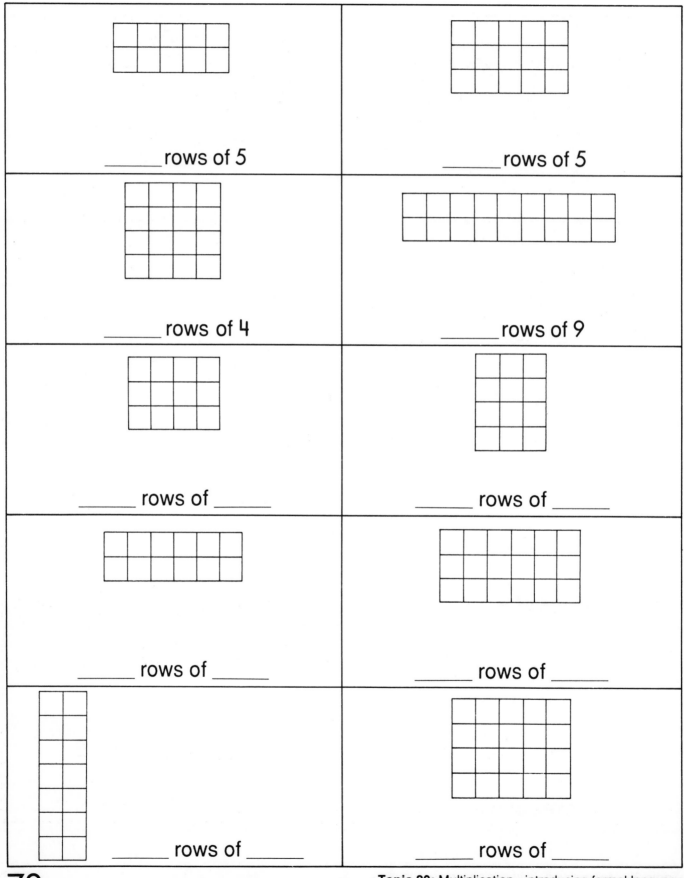

_____ rows of 5

_____ rows of 5

_____ rows of 4

_____ rows of 9

_____ rows of _____

_____ rows of _____

_____ rows of _____

_____ rows of _____

_____ rows of _____

_____ rows of _____

Topic 20: Multiplication - introducing formal language

Name _____

Ring groups of two.
Write the numbers.

3 groups of 2
3 × 2

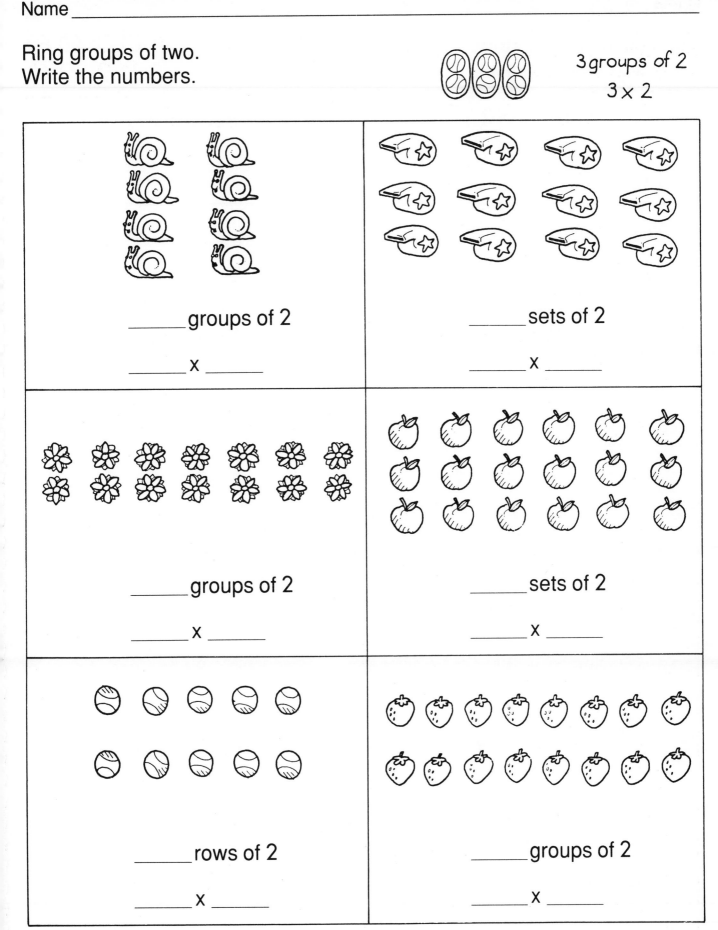

_____ groups of 2

_____ × _____

_____ sets of 2

_____ × _____

_____ groups of 2

_____ × _____

_____ sets of 2

_____ × _____

_____ rows of 2

_____ × _____

_____ groups of 2

_____ × _____

Topic 20: Multiplication - introducing formal language

Name _____

Read each number story.
Draw a picture to match.

2 rows of 4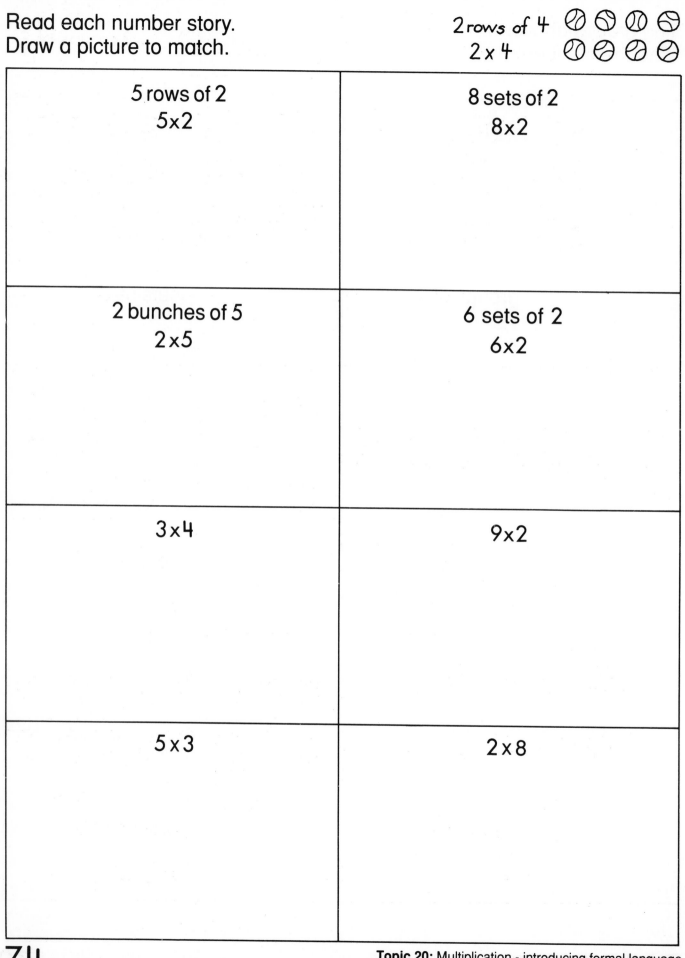
2 x 4

5 rows of 2 5x2	8 sets of 2 8x2
2 bunches of 5 2x5	6 sets of 2 6x2
3x4	9x2
5x3	2x8

Topic 20: Multiplication - introducing formal language

Name _____

Ring the groups.
Write the missing number.
Write the number sentence.

$\underline{3}$ rows of 4.
$3 \times 4 = 12$

_____ sets of 2

_____

_____ groups of 2

_____

_____ sets of 2

_____

_____ rows of 6

_____

_____ groups of 4

_____

_____ rows of 5

_____

_____ rows of 5

_____

_____ sets of 8

_____

Topic 20: Multiplication - introducing formal language

75

Name _____

Draw a picture to match each of these.
Write the missing numbers.
Write a number sentence.

2 rows of five is 10
OOOOO
OOOOO
2x5=10

5 rows of three is 15 _____	7 rows of two is 14 _____
2 sets of seven is _____ _____	4 rows of three is _____ _____
3 rows of four is _____ _____	6 sets of two equals _____ _____
2 groups of eight equals _____ _____	2 rows of nine equals _____ _____

Topic 20: Multiplication - introducing formal language

Name _____

1. Write the correct times in each row.
2. Draw hands on the clocks to match.

2 o'clock	1 hour past 2 o'clock is	2 hours past 2 o'clock is	3 hours past 2 o'clock is
	3 o'clock	_____	_____

5 o'clock	1 hour past 5 o'clock is	2 hours past 5 o'clock is	3 hours past 5 o'clock is
	_____	_____	_____

9 o'clock	1 hour past 9 o'clock is	2 hours past 9 o'clock is	3 hours past 9 o'clock is
	_____	_____	_____

11 o'clock	1 hour past 11 o'clock is	2 hours past 11 o'clock is	3 hours past 11 o'clock is
	_____	_____	_____

12 o'clock	1 hour past 12 o'clock is	2 hours past 12 o'clock is	3 hours past 12 o'clock is
	_____	_____	_____

Topic 21: Time - five-minute intervals

77

Name _____

Put a red mark on each hour hand.
Put a blue mark on each minute hand.
Count by fives to tell the number of minutes past the hour.
Write the missing numbers.

The hour hand is between _____ and _____.

The clock shows _____ minutes past 9.

The hour hand is between _____ and _____.

The clock shows _____ minutes past 8.

The hour hand is between _____ and _____.

The clock shows _____ minutes past 5.

The hour hand is between _____ and _____.

The clock shows _____ minutes past 6.

The hour hand is between _____ and _____.

The clock shows _____ minutes past 10.

The hour hand is between _____ and _____.

The clock shows _____ minutes past 12.

Topic 21: Time - five-minute intervals

Name _____

Draw the minute hand on each clock to show the time.
Write the missing numbers.

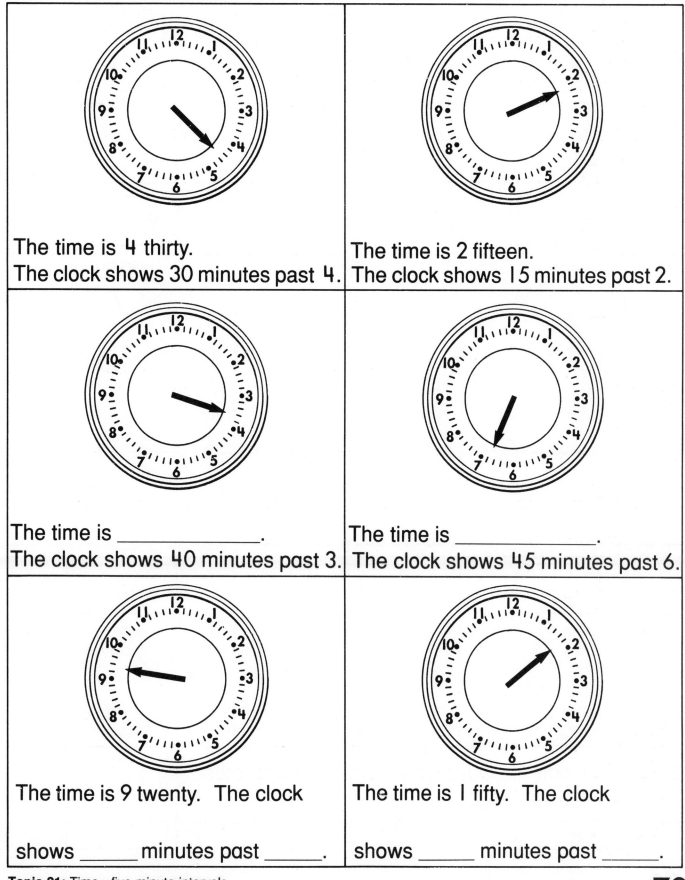

The time is 4 thirty.
The clock shows 30 minutes past 4.

The time is 2 fifteen.
The clock shows 15 minutes past 2.

The time is _____.
The clock shows 40 minutes past 3.

The time is _____.
The clock shows 45 minutes past 6.

The time is 9 twenty. The clock

shows _____ minutes past _____.

The time is 1 fifty. The clock

shows _____ minutes past _____.

Topic 21: Time - five-minute intervals

79

Name _____

1. Count by fives to tell the number of minutes past the hour.
   Write the missing numbers.

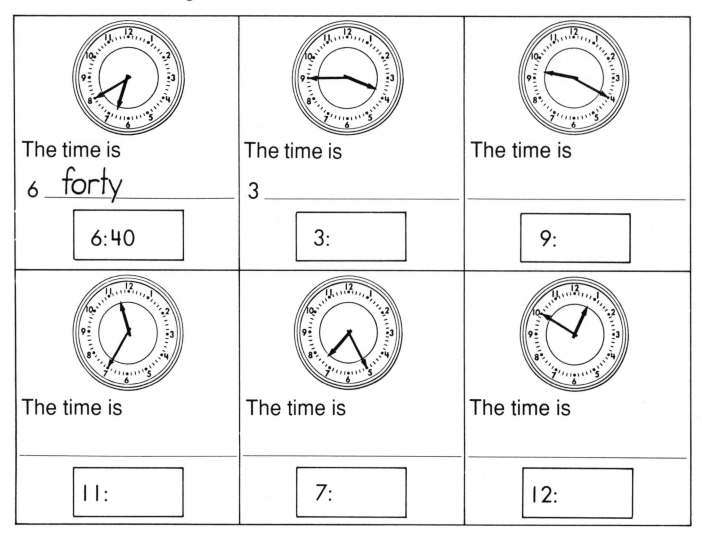

The time is

6 _forty_____

| 6:40 |

The time is

3 _____

| 3: |

The time is

_____

| 9: |

The time is

_____

| 11: |

The time is

_____

| 7: |

The time is

_____

| 12: |

2. Draw hands on each clock to show the time.

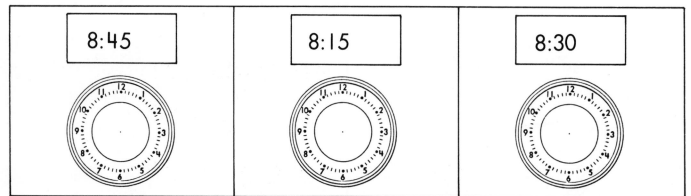

| 8:45 |

| 8:15 |

| 8:30 |

3. Write the times in Question 2 from earliest to latest.

| | | | | |

Topic 21: Time - five-minute intervals

Name _____

Put the correct number of blocks on each picture.
Make 2 equal shares. Draw the blocks.
Write how many in each share.

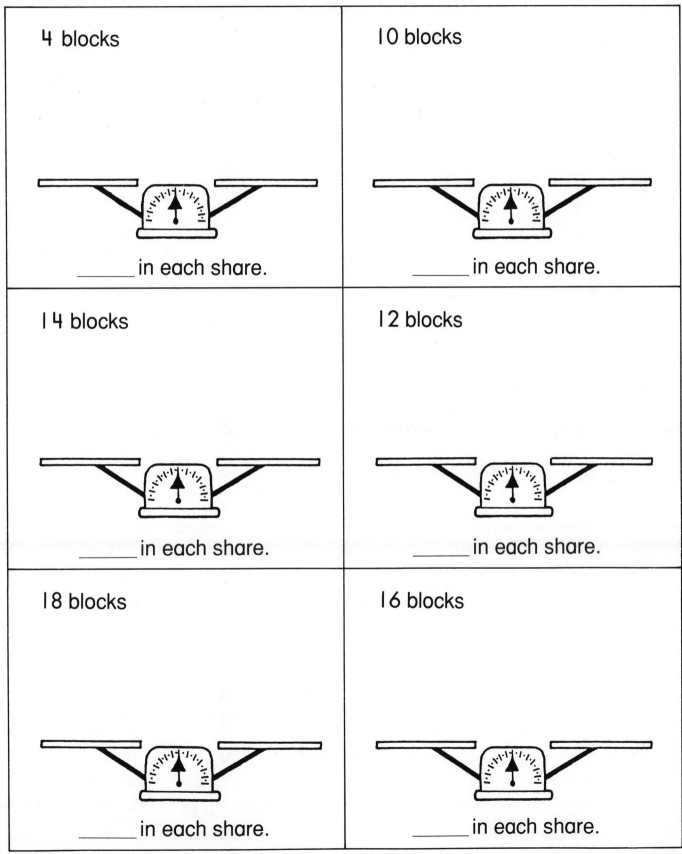

4 blocks

_____ in each share.

10 blocks

_____ in each share.

14 blocks

_____ in each share.

12 blocks

_____ in each share.

18 blocks

_____ in each share.

16 blocks

_____ in each share.

Name _____

Write how many things are in each picture.
Ring groups of two.
Write how many groups you made.

6 blocks

3 groups of two

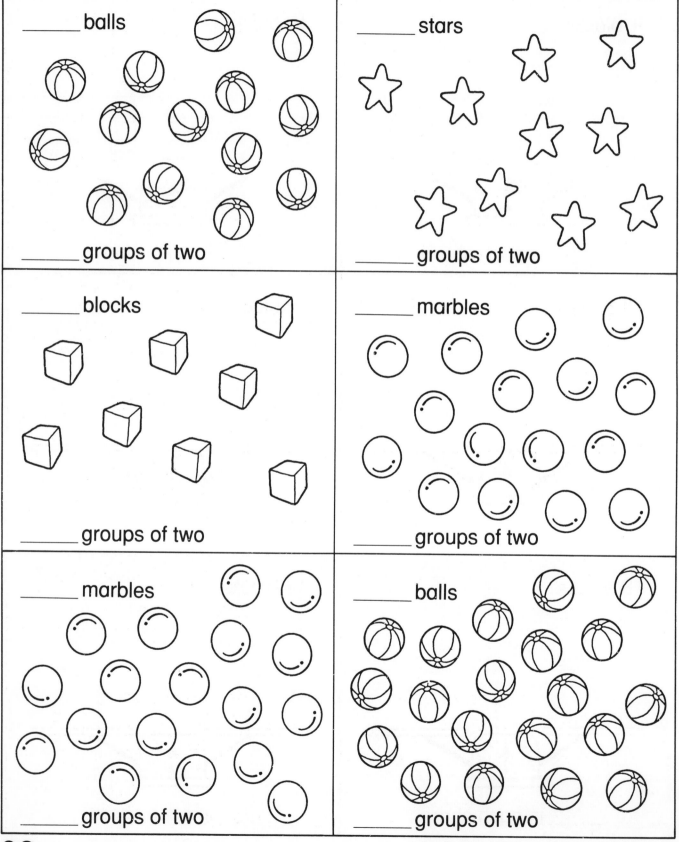

_____ balls

_____ groups of two

_____ stars

_____ groups of two

_____ blocks

_____ groups of two

_____ marbles

_____ groups of two

_____ marbles

_____ groups of two

_____ balls

_____ groups of two

Topic 22: Division - using informal language

Name _____

Write how many things are in each picture.
Ring groups of three.
Write how many groups you made.

_____ blocks

_____ groups of three

_____ blocks

_____ groups of three

_____ stars

_____ groups of three

_____ marbles

_____ groups of three

_____ blocks

_____ groups of three

_____ balls

_____ groups of three

_____ balls

_____ groups of three

_____ blocks

_____ groups of three

Name _____

Put the correct number of blocks on each picture.
Divide the blocks into equal shares.
Draw the blocks in each share. Write the number in each share.

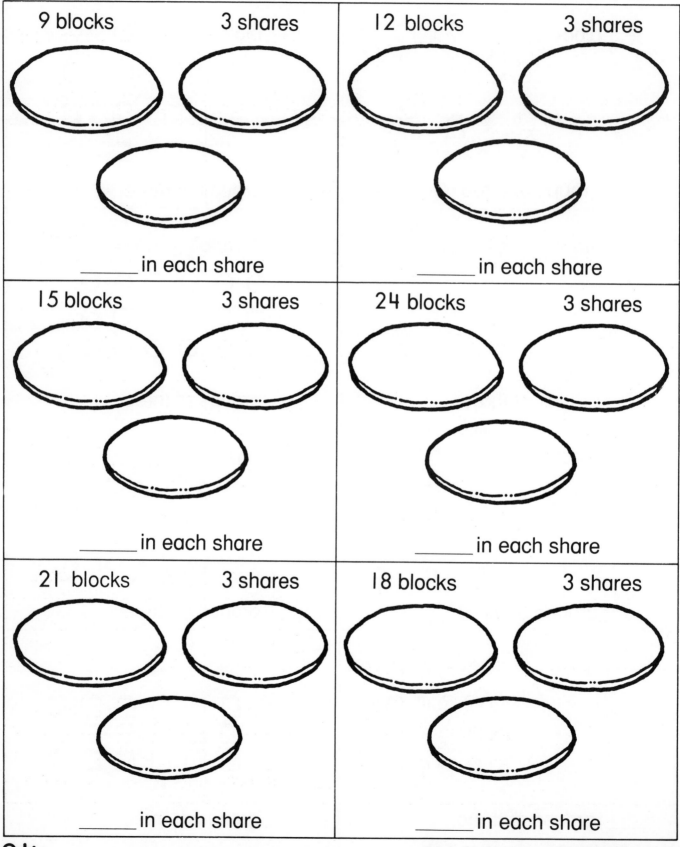

9 blocks   3 shares

_____ in each share

12 blocks   3 shares

_____ in each share

15 blocks   3 shares

_____ in each share

24 blocks   3 shares

_____ in each share

21 blocks   3 shares

_____ in each share

18 blocks   3 shares

_____ in each share

84

Name _____

1. Kick a ball from a marked spot on in the playground.
   Estimate the distance in paces. Then check by pacing.
   Estimate the distance in meters. Then check
   with a meter stick.

My estimate	My measure
_____ paces	_____ paces
_____ meters	_____ meters

2. How far can you throw the things listed below?
   Fill in the table.

What did you throw?	My estimate	My measure
bean bag	_____ paces	_____ paces
	_____ meters	_____ meters
crumpled newspaper ball	_____ paces	_____ paces
	_____ meters	_____ meters
beach ball	_____ paces	_____ paces
	_____ meters	_____ meters
tennis ball	_____ paces	_____ paces
	_____ meters	_____ meters
baseball	_____ paces	_____ paces
	_____ meters	_____ meters

Name _____

1. The paintbrush is _____ centimeters long.
2. Cut a strip of string 20 centimeters long. Compare it with some things in your classroom. Fill in this table.

less than 20 centimeters	about 20 centimeters	more than 20 centimeters

3. Estimate, then measure, each of these to the nearest centimeter.

You can mark the length on paper first.

	My estimate	My measure
length of my index finger		
length of my hand		
length of my right shoe		
length of my left shoe		
length of a softball bat		
width of the doorway		
width of this page		
height of my desk or table		

Topic 23: Measurement - relating units involving length

Name _____

1. Find the objects listed in the table.
   Measure each line of objects with a meter stick or a tape measure.
   Record each length in the table below.
   Figure out how much less than one meter each length is.

objects end-to-end	
8 orange rods	_____ centimeters long. This is _____ centimeters less than 1 meter.
8 blue rods	_____ centimeters long. This is _____ centimeters less than 1 meter.
8 brown rods	_____ centimeters long. This is _____ centimeters less than 1 meter.
5 envelopes	_____ centimeters long. This is _____ centimeters _____ than 1 meter.
6 school pencils	_____ centimeters long. This is _____ centimeters _____ than 1 meter.
3 activity books	_____ centimeters long. This is _____ centimeters _____ than 1 meter.

2. Make these measurements. Record each length on the table below.

5 handspans	_____ centimeters long. This is _____ centimeters less than 1 meter.
5 footprints	_____ centimeters long. This is _____ centimeters less than 1 meter.
1 pace	_____ centimeters long. This is _____ centimeters less than 1 meter.

Topic 23: Measurement - relating units involving length

Name _____

Draw or paste pictures of coins to
show each price in two different ways.
Write the number of coins you used.

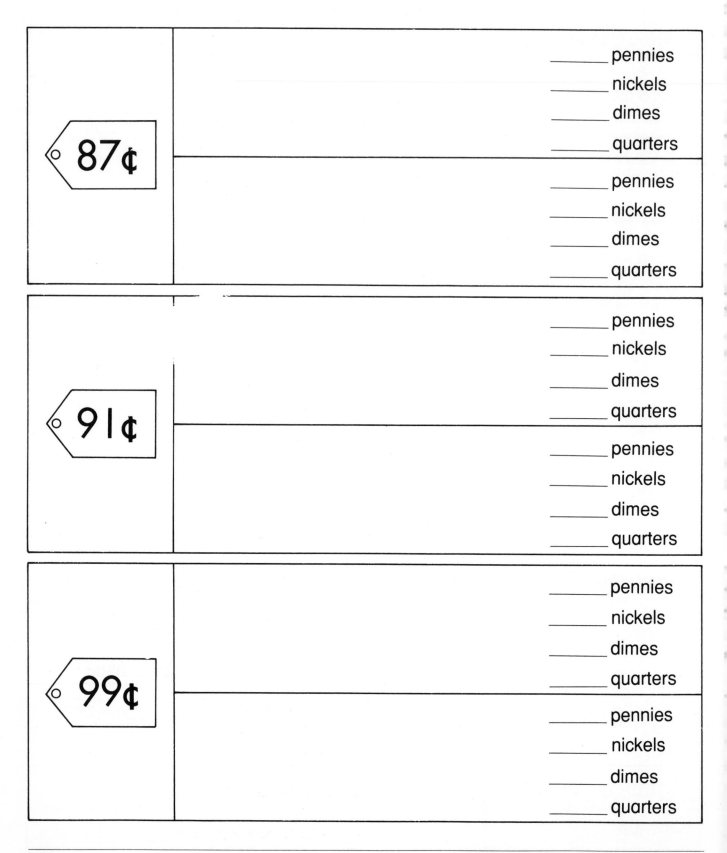

87¢

_____ pennies
_____ nickels
_____ dimes
_____ quarters

_____ pennies
_____ nickels
_____ dimes
_____ quarters

91¢

_____ pennies
_____ nickels
_____ dimes
_____ quarters

_____ pennies
_____ nickels
_____ dimes
_____ quarters

99¢

_____ pennies
_____ nickels
_____ dimes
_____ quarters

_____ pennies
_____ nickels
_____ dimes
_____ quarters

Topic 24: Extending the Addition Algorithm

Name _____

1. Draw or paste pictures of coins to
   show one dollar in four different ways.
   Write the number of coins you used.

is the same as

_____ pennies	_____ pennies	_____ pennies	_____ pennies
_____ nickels	_____ nickels	_____ nickels	_____ nickels
_____ dimes	_____ dimes	_____ dimes	_____ dimes
_____ quarters	_____ quarters	_____ quarters	_____ quarters

2. Use coins to help answer these questions.

   $1 take away 1¢ is _____ $1 take away 5¢ is _____

   $1 take away 10¢ is _____ $1 take away 25¢ is _____

Topic 24: Extending the Addition Algorithm

Name _____

Write how many tens and ones you see in each picture.
If you can, ring 10 ones to make another ten.
Fill in a new label.

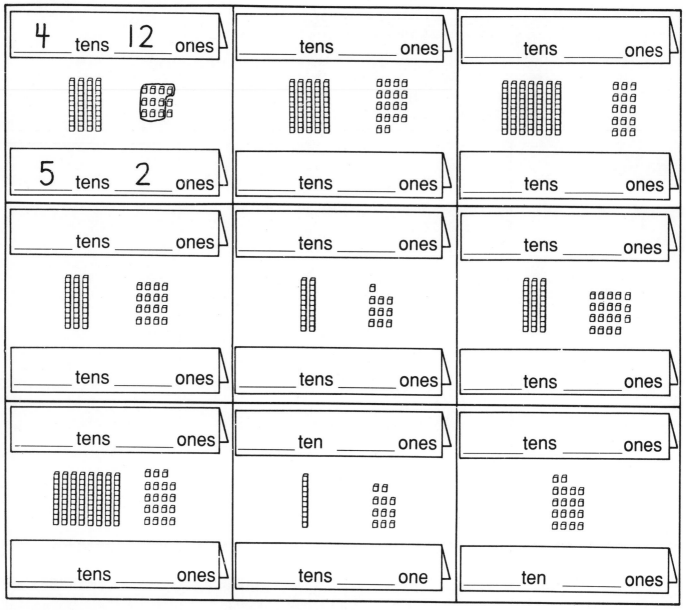

_4_ tens _12_ ones

_____ tens _____ ones

_____ tens _____ ones

_5_ tens _2_ ones

_____ tens _____ ones

_____ tens _____ ones

_____ tens _____ ones

_____ tens _____ ones

_____ tens _____ ones

_____ tens _____ ones

_____ tens _____ ones

_____ tens _____ ones

_____ tens _____ ones

_____ ten _____ ones

_____ tens _____ ones

_____ tens _____ ones

_____ tens _____ one

_____ ten _____ ones

2. Figure out if you can trade 10 ones for 1 ten.
   If you can, fill in the new numbers.

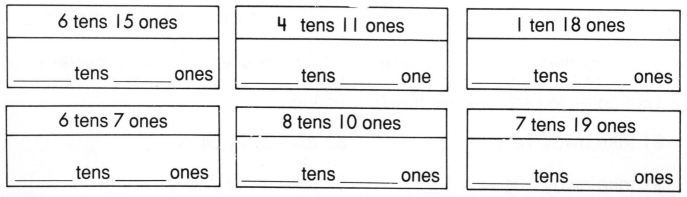

6 tens 15 ones	4 tens 11 ones	1 ten 18 ones
_____ tens _____ ones	_____ tens _____ one	_____ tens _____ ones

6 tens 7 ones	8 tens 10 ones	7 tens 19 ones
_____ tens _____ ones	_____ tens _____ ones	_____ tens _____ ones

Topic 24: Extending the Addition Algorithm

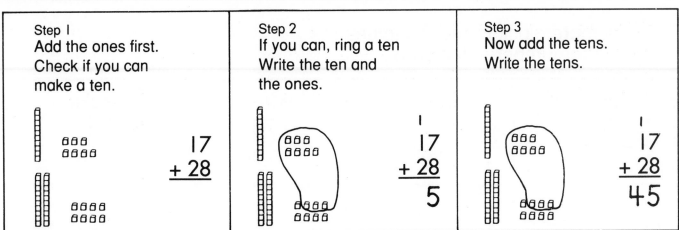

Step 1	Step 2	Step 3
Add the ones first. Check if you can make a ten.	If you can, ring a ten Write the ten and the ones.	Now add the tens. Write the tens.

Step 1:
$$\begin{array}{r} 17 \\ + 28 \\ \hline \end{array}$$

Step 2:
$$\begin{array}{r} {\scriptstyle 1} \\ 17 \\ + 28 \\ \hline 5 \end{array}$$

Step 3:
$$\begin{array}{r} {\scriptstyle 1} \\ 17 \\ + 28 \\ \hline 45 \end{array}$$

Add these.
Use the picture of blocks to help.

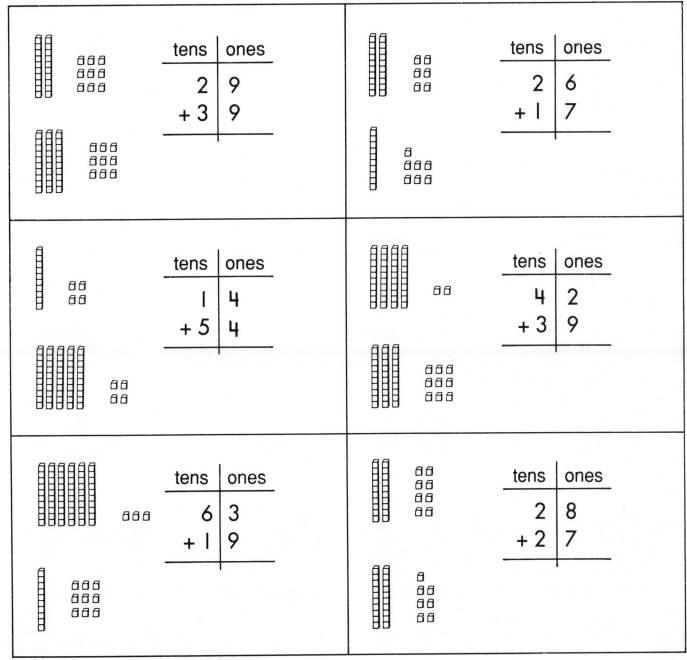

tens	ones
2	9
+ 3	9

tens	ones
2	6
+ 1	7

tens	ones
1	4
+ 5	4

tens	ones
4	2
+ 3	9

tens	ones
6	3
+ 1	9

tens	ones
2	8
+ 2	7

Topic 24: Extending the Addition Algorithm

91

Name _____

1. Draw more blocks in each picture.
Write the number you added.

Make 78 in all.	Make 78 in all.	Make 78 in all.	Make 78 in all.
I added	I added	I added	I added
_____	_____	_____	_____

2. Cross off the correct number of blocks in each picture.
Write the number that is left.

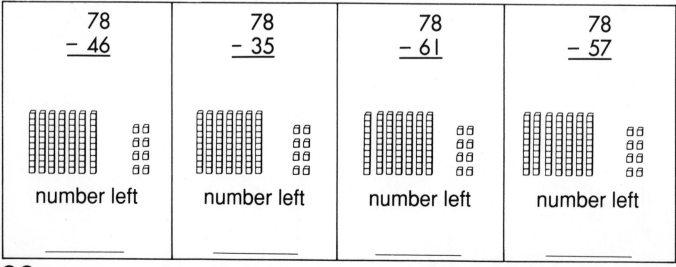

78 − 46	78 − 35	78 − 61	78 − 57
number left	number left	number left	number left
_____	_____	_____	_____

1. Add enough coins to the starting amount to equal the total amount.
   Draw or paste pictures of coins.

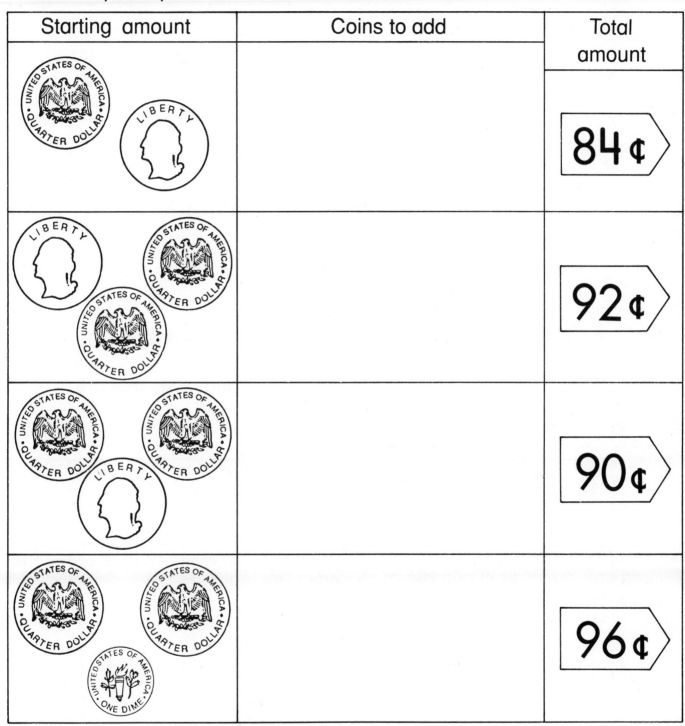

Starting amount	Coins to add	Total amount
		84¢
		92¢
		90¢
		96¢

2. Write the answers. You may use coins to help.

16	62	58	76	59
+ 34	+ 13	+ 17	+ 9	+ 16

Topic 24: Extending the Addition Algorithm

1. Draw some different shapes with 4 square corners.

2. Color the shapes in this design in this way.
   • red if the shape has 4 square corners and all sides are the same length
   • green if the shape has 4 square corners and sides that are <u>not</u> the same length

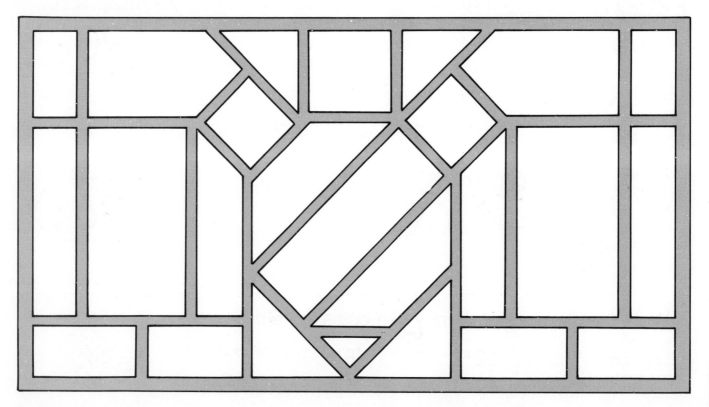

3. Put a check on each shape that has no square corners.

Topic 25: Investigating Plane Shapes

Name _____

1. Put a piece of string
   around a hundreds block .
   Measure the length of the string. 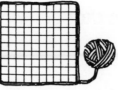 The length of
   the string is

   _____ centimeters

2. Measure the length of each side of a hundreds block.

top	_____ centimeters wide
bottom	_____ centimeters wide
left side	_____ centimeters long
right side	_____ centimeters long
Total	_____

3. Add the 4 lengths in Question 2.

   What did you find out? _____

   _____

4. Measure the sides of this envelope and fill in the table below.

top _____ centimeters   left side _____ centimeters

bottom _____ centimeters   right side _____ centimeters

distance around the envelope _____ centimeters

1. Draw some shapes that balance.

2. Draw lines to show where these shapes balance.

3. Color squares to make these designs balance.

Name _____

Draw lines across each shape from corner to corner.
Use a different color for each line.
Write the numbers.

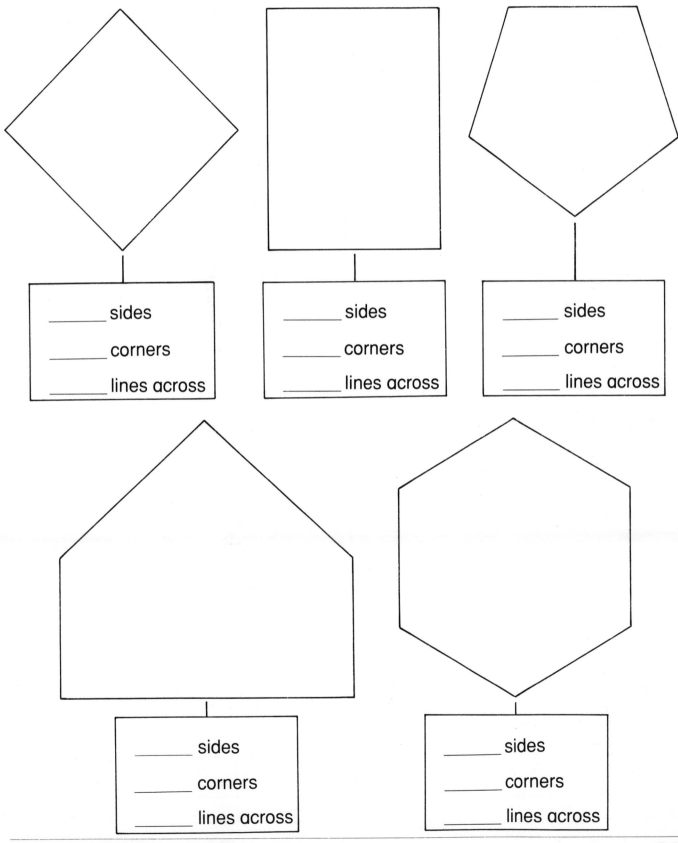

_____ sides

_____ corners

_____ lines across

_____ sides

_____ corners

_____ lines across

_____ sides

_____ corners

_____ lines across

_____ sides

_____ corners

_____ lines across

_____ sides

_____ corners

_____ lines across

1. Draw dots on the folder for the subtraction fact.
   Write two addition facts.
   Write the answer to the subtraction fact.

$$\begin{array}{r}13\\-4\\\hline 9\end{array}$$ [13] $$\begin{array}{r}4\\+9\\\hline 13\end{array}$$ $$\begin{array}{r}9\\+4\\\hline 13\end{array}$$

$$\begin{array}{r}14\\-5\\\hline\end{array}$$ [14] ___ ___ ___	$$\begin{array}{r}16\\-9\\\hline\end{array}$$ [16] ___ ___ ___
$$\begin{array}{r}13\\-8\\\hline\end{array}$$ [13] ___ ___ ___	$$\begin{array}{r}12\\-4\\\hline\end{array}$$ [12] ___ ___ ___

2. Write two addition facts to help answer each subtraction fact.

$$\begin{array}{r}12\\-8\\\hline\end{array}$$ ___ ___	$$\begin{array}{r}16\\-7\\\hline\end{array}$$ ___ ___	$$\begin{array}{r}10\\-4\\\hline\end{array}$$ ___ ___
$$\begin{array}{r}14\\-9\\\hline\end{array}$$ ___ ___	$$\begin{array}{r}13\\-5\\\hline\end{array}$$ ___ ___	$$\begin{array}{r}13\\-9\\\hline\end{array}$$ ___ ___

Topic 26: More Subtraction Strategies

Name _____

1. Write two addition facts and two subtraction facts for each domino.

$$\begin{array}{cccc} 8 & 7 & 15 & 15 \\ +7 & +8 & -7 & -8 \\ \hline 15 & 15 & 8 & 7 \end{array}$$

___ ___ ___ ___	___ ___ ___ ___
___ ___ ___ ___	___ ___ ___ ___
___ ___ ___ ___	___ ___ ___ ___

2. Write two addition facts to help answer each subtraction fact.

$\begin{array}{r} 16 \\ -9 \\ \hline \end{array}$ ___ ___	$\begin{array}{r} 10 \\ -6 \\ \hline \end{array}$ ___ ___	$\begin{array}{r} 14 \\ -5 \\ \hline \end{array}$ ___ ___
$\begin{array}{r} 13 \\ -8 \\ \hline \end{array}$ ___ ___	$\begin{array}{r} 13 \\ -4 \\ \hline \end{array}$ ___ ___	$\begin{array}{r} 15 \\ -4 \\ \hline \end{array}$ ___ ___

Name _____

1. Write in the bottom boxes how many tens and ones you see.
   Trade one ten for 10 ones by crossing out a ten and drawing 10 ones.
   Fill in the top boxes to show how many tens and ones you have now.

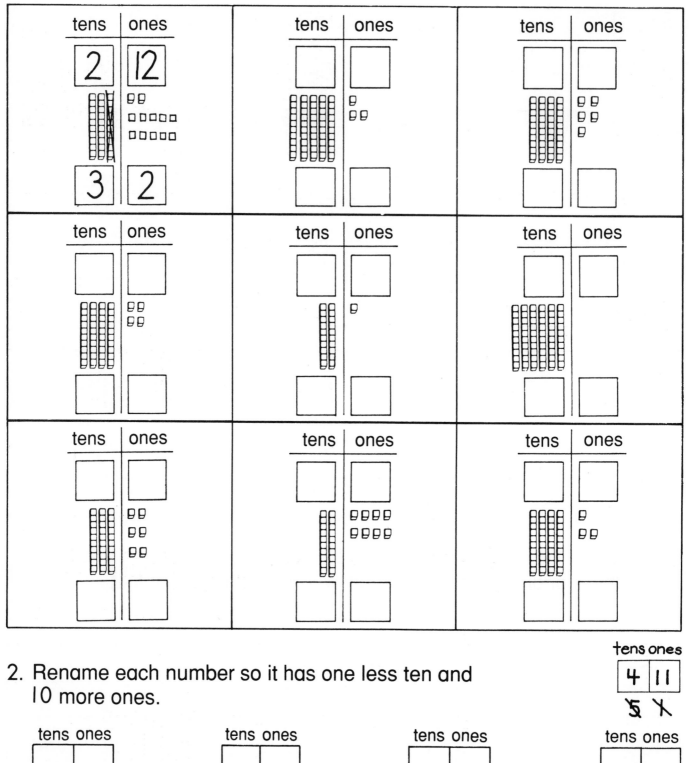

2. Rename each number so it has one less ten and
   10 more ones.

tens ones
82

tens ones
63

tens ones
94

tens ones
50

Topic 27: Extending the Subtraction Algorithm

Name _____

1. Use blocks to "act out" steps 1, 2, and 3.

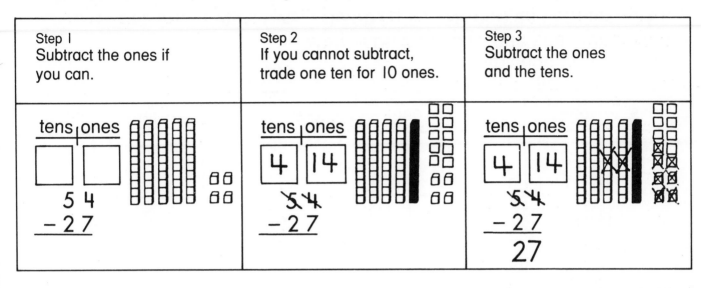

Step 1 Subtract the ones if you can.	Step 2 If you cannot subtract, trade one ten for 10 ones.	Step 3 Subtract the ones and the tens.
tens ones [ ] [ ] 5 4 − 2 7	tens ones 4 14 5̸ 4̸ − 2 7	tens ones 4 14 5̸ 4̸ − 2 7 2 7

2. Use the steps in Question 1 to find the answer for each of these. You may use blocks.

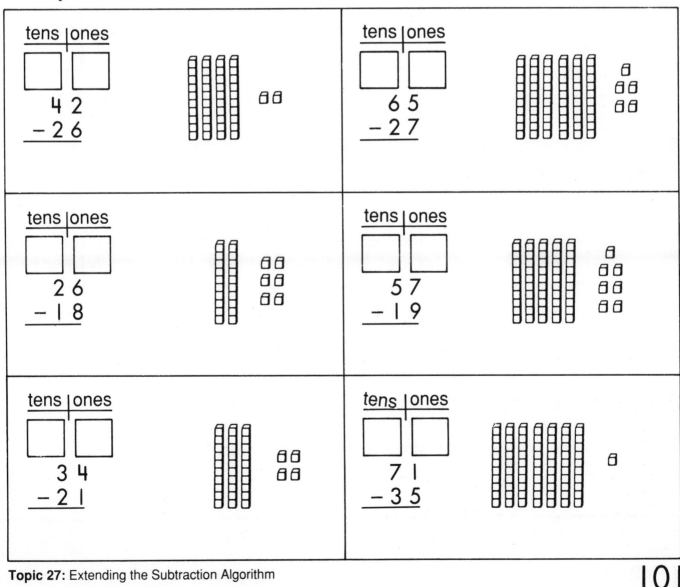

tens ones
[ ] [ ]
4 2
− 2 6

tens ones
[ ] [ ]
6 5
− 2 7

tens ones
[ ] [ ]
2 6
− 1 8

tens ones
[ ] [ ]
5 7
− 1 9

tens ones
[ ] [ ]
3 4
− 2 1

tens ones
[ ] [ ]
7 1
− 3 5

Name _____

1. Try to subtract the ones in each of these.
   If you can't, trade one ten for 10 ones. Then write in the boxes
   how many tens and ones you have now.
   Subtract the ones and tens.

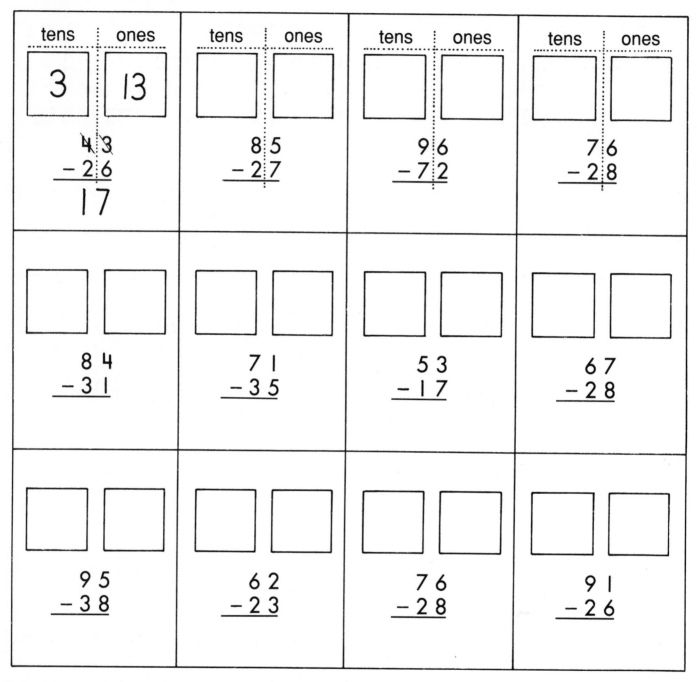

tens	ones		tens	ones		tens	ones		tens	ones
3	13									

```
  4 3          8 5          9 6          7 6
- 2 6        - 2 7        - 7 2        - 2 8
  1 7
```

```
  8 4          7 1          5 3          6 7
- 3 1        - 3 5        - 1 7        - 2 8
```

```
  9 5          6 2          7 6          9 1
- 3 8        - 2 3        - 2 8        - 2 6
```

2. Write the answers. Check first to see if you need to regroup.

```
  76           87           92           81           60
- 28         - 35         - 36         - 35         - 25
```

Topic 27: Extending the Subtraction Algorithm

Name _____

1. Cross out coins to find the answers.
   Write the answers.

$$\begin{array}{r} 44 \\ -13 \\ \hline \end{array}$$

$$\begin{array}{r} 48 \\ -27 \\ \hline \end{array}$$

$$\begin{array}{r} 62 \\ -37 \\ \hline \end{array}$$

$$\begin{array}{r} 91 \\ -35 \\ \hline \end{array}$$

2. For each starting number, draw a picture of coins. Cross out coins to find the answer. Write the answer.

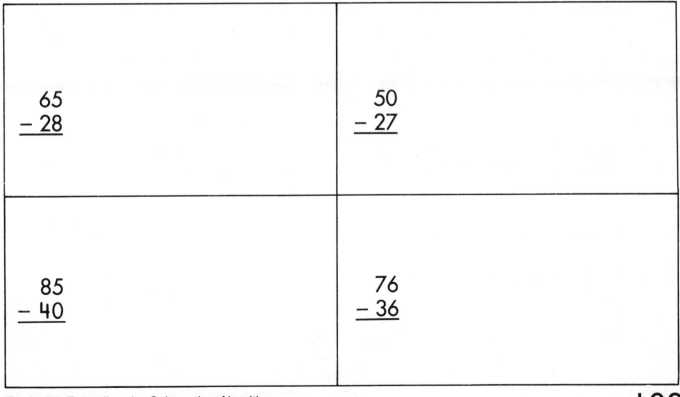

$$\begin{array}{r} 65 \\ -28 \\ \hline \end{array}$$

$$\begin{array}{r} 50 \\ -27 \\ \hline \end{array}$$

$$\begin{array}{r} 85 \\ -40 \\ \hline \end{array}$$

$$\begin{array}{r} 76 \\ -36 \\ \hline \end{array}$$

Name _____

1. Use tens and ones blocks to help answer the questions.

Rose 96 centimeters	Sunflower 75 centimeters	Lily 87 centimeters	Daffodil 36 centimeters	Daisy 49 centimeters	Petunia 25 centimeters	Marigold 32 centimeters

How much taller is the lily than the daffodil? _____	How much more does the petunia have to grow to be the same height as the daisy? _____
Find the difference in height between the marigold and the sunflower. _____	How much more does the petunia have to grow to reach 75 centimeters? _____
The fence is 80 centimeters high. How much shorter is the daffodil? _____	How much taller is the rose than the daisy? _____

2. Write the answers.

87	49	75	75	80	96
− 36	− 25	− 32	− 25	− 36	− 49

Name _____

1. Color one equal part of each shape.

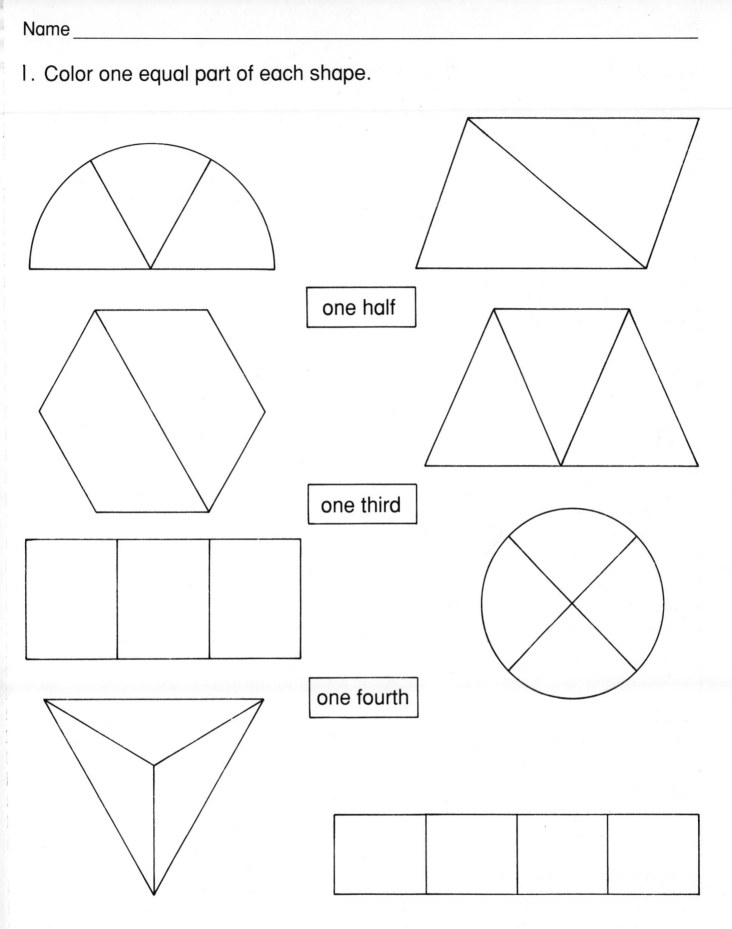

one half

one third

one fourth

2. Draw a line to join each shape to the fraction name that matches.

Name _____

1. Write the number of equal parts you see in each picture.
   Color one of the parts.
   Write the fraction name that tells how much of each shape you colored.

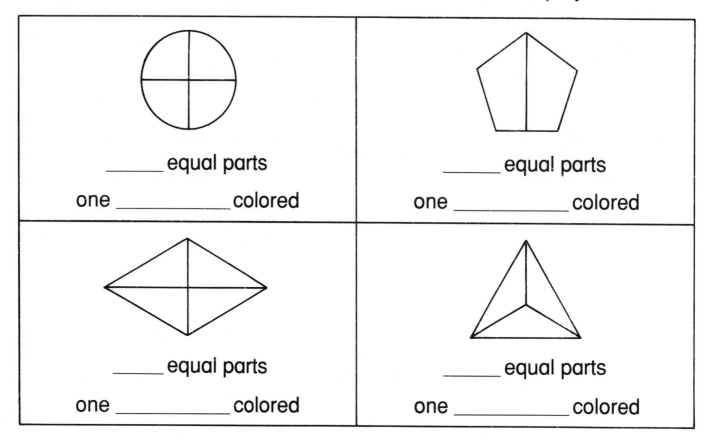

_____ equal parts

one _____ colored

_____ equal parts

one _____ colored

_____ equal parts

one _____ colored

_____ equal parts

one _____ colored

2. Color each shape to show the fraction.

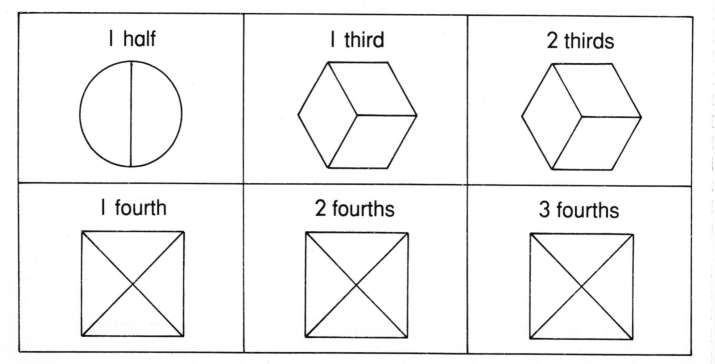

| 1 half | 1 third | 2 thirds |
| 1 fourth | 2 fourths | 3 fourths |

Topic 28: Fractions and Area - halves, thirds, fourths

Name _____

1. Color one equal part of each shape.
   Then draw a line to join each shape to the fraction that matches.

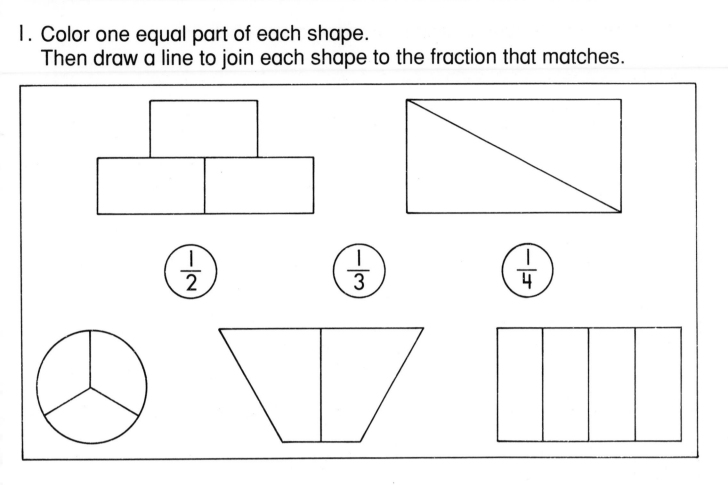

2. Color two equal parts of each shape.
   Then draw a line to join each shape to the fraction that matches.

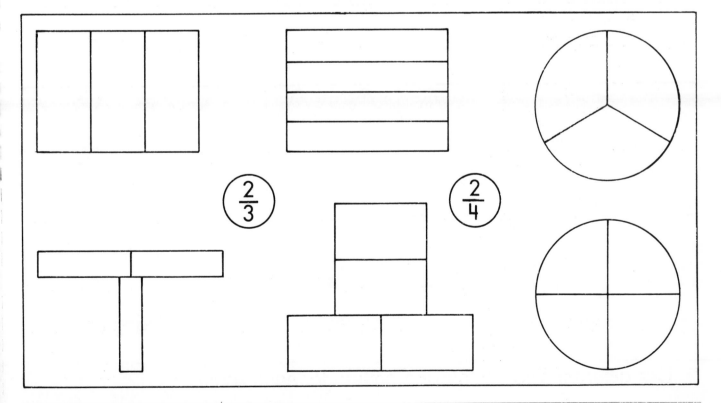

Name _____

1. Write how many tiles have been used to cover each floor.

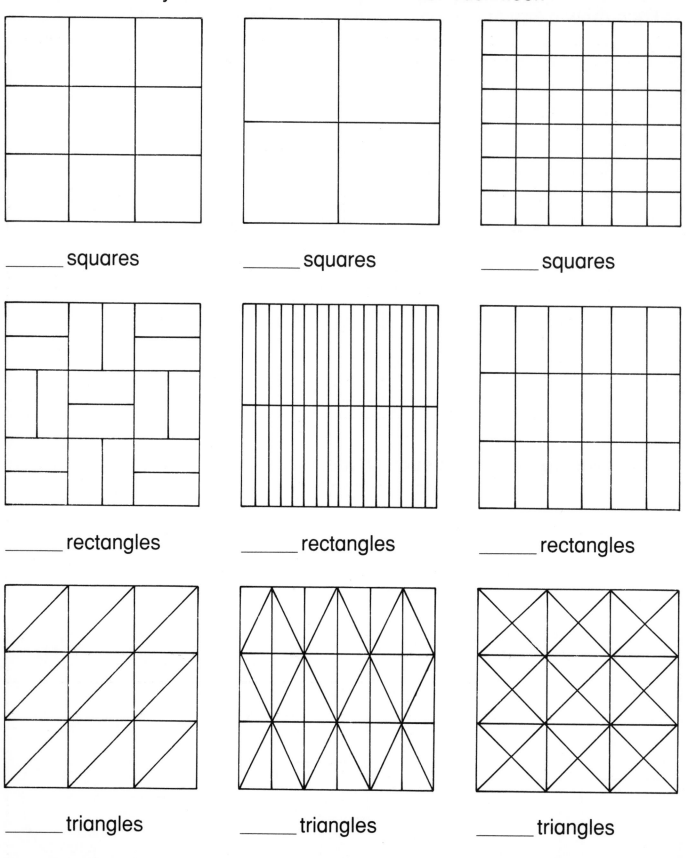

_____ squares   _____ squares   _____ squares

_____ rectangles   _____ rectangles   _____ rectangles

_____ triangles   _____ triangles   _____ triangles

2. Use different colors to make a pattern for each floor.

108   **Topic 28**: Fractions and Area - halves, thirds, fourths

Name _____

Draw vegetables in rows to show each sentence.
Then write the answer.

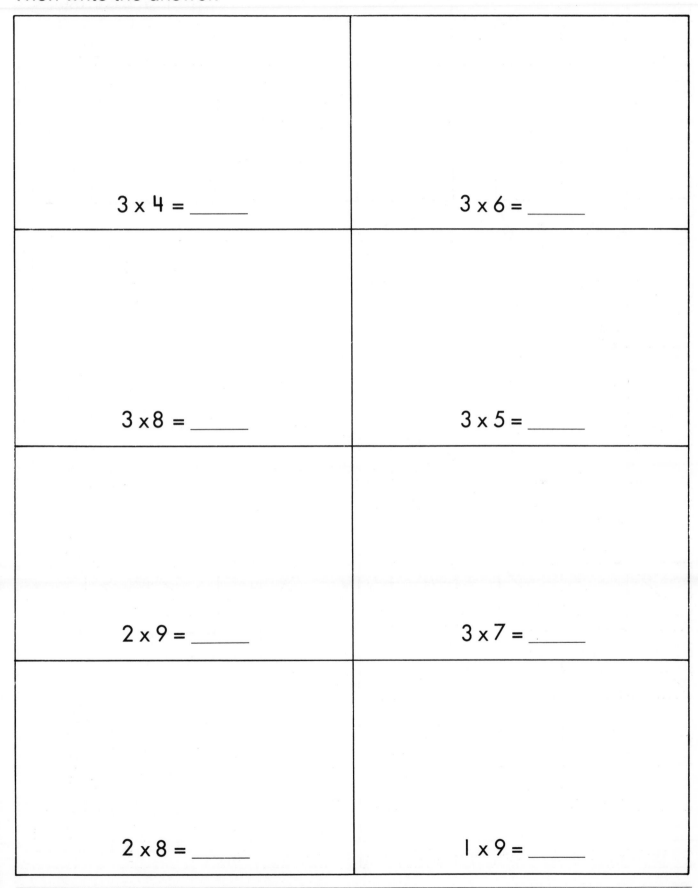

3 x 4 = _____

3 x 6 = _____

3 x 8 = _____

3 x 5 = _____

2 x 9 = _____

3 x 7 = _____

2 x 8 = _____

1 x 9 = _____

Name _____

Draw pegs on the empty board to show what you would
see when the other board is turned sideways.
Then write both of the multiplication facts.

You can use
a pegboard
to help.

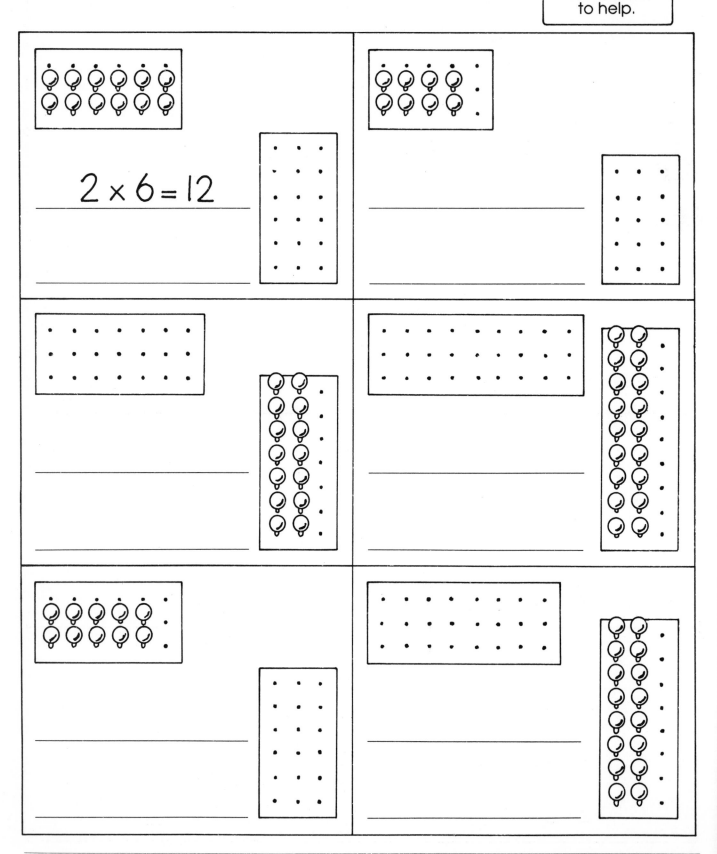

$2 \times 6 = 12$

Name _____

1. Write a multiplication sentence in words to match each picture.
   Then write a multiplication number sentence.

⬚ dots	__2 fives are 10__ __2×5 =10__
⬚ dots	_____ _____
⬚ dots	_____ _____
⬚ dots	_____ _____
⬚ dots	_____ _____
⬚ dots	_____ _____
⬚ dots	_____ _____

2. Write the answers.

Buy 8 ▯.
Pay 5¢ for each.
How much do they
cost altogether? _____

Read 5 books a month.
How many books altogether
in 5 months?

_____

A ▱ is 5 inches high.
Stack 7 ▱.
How high is the stack? _____

A ▯ weighs
5 pounds.
What is the weight of

6 ▯ ? _____

Topic 29: Extending Multiplication and Division

Name _____

1. Write the answers to these.

$2 \times 6 =$ _____ $4 \times 5 =$ _____ $9 \times 2 =$ _____ $5 \times 10 =$ _____

$5 \times 7 =$ _____ $5 \times 8 =$ _____ $5 \times 3 =$ _____ $7 \times 2 =$ _____

2. What is the missing number?
   Write it on the finger.

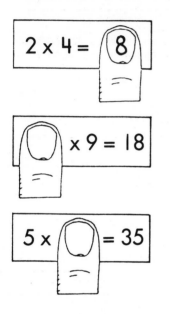

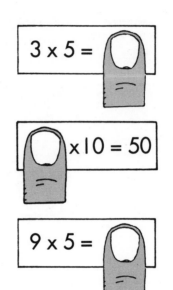

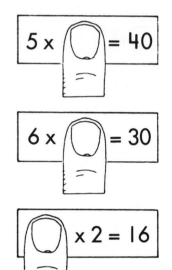

$2 \times 4 =$ 8

$3 \times 5 =$

$5 \times$ $= 40$

$\times 9 = 18$

$\times 10 = 50$

$6 \times$ $= 30$

$5 \times$ $= 35$

$9 \times 5 =$

$\times 2 = 16$

3. Draw a picture for each of these. Use your blocks first.
   Then write a multiplication fact for each picture.

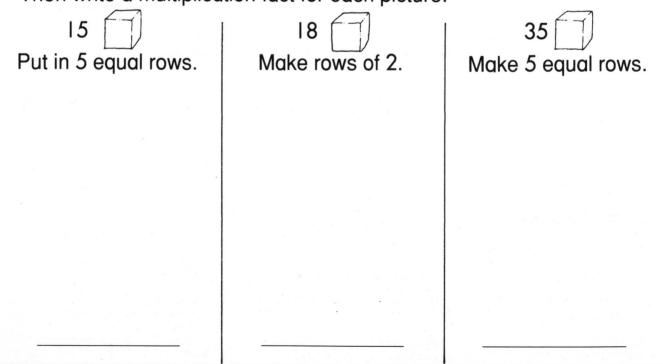

15   Put in 5 equal rows.

18   Make rows of 2.

35   Make 5 equal rows.

_____   _____   _____

Topic 29: Extending Multiplication and Division